942.05 Southworth, John
Sou          Van Duyn

        Monarch and
          conspirators

| DATE | | | |
|---|---|---|---|
| MAR 1 '77 | | | |
| | | | |
| | | | |
| | | | |
| | | | |
| | | | |
| | | | |
| | | | |
| | | | |
| | | | |
| | | | |

# MONARCH AND CONSPIRATORS
## The Wives and Woes of Henry VIII

Jane Seymour     Anne of Cleves     Catherine Howard
Catherine Parr     HENRY VIII     Anne Boleyn
Catherine of Aragon

# MONARCH AND CONSPIRATORS

## The Wives and Woes of Henry VIII

BY

## John Van Duyn Southworth

Crown Publishers, Inc., New York

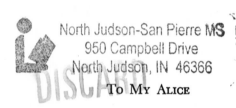
To My Alice

ACKNOWLEDGMENT

*The author gratefully acknowledges the use of
the following illustrations:*
*The Granger Collection: 65, 85, 89, 96, 171, 219*
*Historical Picture Service, Chicago: frontispiece, 5, 37,
48, 59, 81, 100, 111, 133, 157, 194, jacket*

Printed in the United States of America
Library of Congress Catalog Card Number: 72-92387
ISBN: 0-517-50261-5
Published simultaneously in Canada by
General Publishing Company Limited
First Printing

The text of this book is set in 11 pt. Electra.
The illustrations are black and white halftones.

# CONTENTS

# 1
# PLANTAGENET FOREBEARS

ICHARD PLANTAGENET, Duke of Gloucester, was a member of the English House of York. For twenty-eight years, his family had been fighting a war against the rival House of Lancaster for the right to wear the crown of England. The badge, or symbol, of the House of York was a white rose; that of the House of Lancaster was a red rose. Hence, the bloody struggle between these two embattled families came to be known as the Wars of the Roses. During most of the period of the wars, the House of York managed to hold the crown.

In 1483—the twenty-eighth year of the war—King Edward IV, of the House of York, died, leaving the crown to his twelve-year-old son Edward, who thus became King Edward V. Edward was never crowned. Though he had become king when his father died, the real power had been given to his uncle, Richard Plantagenet, who was to rule until Edward was old enough to assume the responsibilities of being king.

Richard was happy to have the powers of king, but he had no intention of giving them up, then or later, to his brother's son. Instead, he had Edward locked up in the grim Tower of London, saying that he would be safer there until the time of his coronation. Soon Edward's younger brother, Prince Richard, joined him as a prisoner in the Tower. With the boys out of the way, their uncle quietly took full control of the government.

Richard Plantagenet was a strange man. His body was deformed—a fact which gave him his nickname of Richard Crouchback—and his mind was as twisted as his body. When Earl Rivers and Sir Richard Grey—the young king's uncle and half brother —objected to what he was doing, he had them arrested and confined in a castle. Lord William Hastings, a powerful nobleman who had been a close friend of King Edward IV, learned of Richard's plans, but he was unable to interfere. Richard had him seized at a meeting and immediately put to death in a courtyard outside, refusing even to let him know of the charges against him. Richard, meanwhile, had some of his assistants quietly spread the lie that King Edward IV and the boys' mother, Elizabeth Woodville, had never been married, which would have made the boys illegitimate and thus unfit for kingship. He even had a prominent clergyman, Dr. Shaw, preach a sermon on the subject, taking for his text a passage from The Book of Wisdom in the Old Testament: "Bastard slips shall not strike deep roots." It was Richard's hope that these maneuvers would lead the members of the Council and of Parliament to reject the boys and to ask him to be king.

It did not work precisely as planned. Too many prominent people were still suspicious of Richard Plantagenet and wanted his nephews released and King Edward V crowned. Suddenly, this became impossible. The boys were found dead in the Tower, but without a mark on them. It is assumed, though it was never legally proved, that their uncle sent men to the Tower who quietly smothered them. Richard then proclaimed himself King Richard III.

Among the Lancastrians who had fled from England in fear for their lives was a nobleman named Henry Tudor, Earl of Richmond. Gathering an army of about five thousand men, the earl crossed from France, landing on the coast of Wales and advancing eastward into England. King Richard quickly gathered a force of fifteen thousand and advanced to meet him. The armies came together at Bosworth Field, in central England.

One would have thought that King Richard III would have no difficulty in winning the battle, since his army was about three times the size of that being led by the Earl of Richmond. Many in the royal forces had been summoned against their wills, and they were not devoted to Richard's cause. Even before the battle began, one large unit of troops under Sir William Stanley abandoned the king's army and joined his enemies. Early in the battle, a second group, under the Earl of Northumberland, did the same.

When King Richard III saw that his army was deserting him, he sensed that his cause was lost. "Treason!" he shouted. "Treason!" Then, drawing his sword, he dashed into the thick of the fighting, seeking to find and to cut down his principal enemy, Henry Tudor, Earl of Richmond. He did not succeed. The first two men to oppose him fell down before his sword blows, but as he neared his rival he was himself cut down and killed. The crown of England fell from his head and came to rest beside a hawthorn bush in the field. Sir William Stanley found it and presented it to the victorious Henry Tudor.

After thirty years, the Wars of the Roses were over. On this day—August 22, 1485—peace returned to England. Soon Henry Tudor, Earl of Richmond, would be crowned and would become King Henry VII. In a little less than six years, he would become the father of the royal personage about whom this book is written.

King Henry VII began his reign under very grave disadvantages. When his army had faced that of King Richard III at Bosworth Field, he had been merely an earl who had lost most of his possessions fourteen years before, when he had fled to Brittany, on the French coast. Nor had he a very good claim to the throne, for there were others in England whose ancestry was much closer to the royal family line than was his. Even when the battle was over, with King Richard III dead and the crown in Henry's hands, his claim to the throne was slight, and his wealth was totally inadequate for meeting royal expenses.

Support was needed: personal support, which would put the people solidly behind him as a popular king; dynastic support, which would strengthen his claim to the crown and that of his descendants; and financial support, which would make it possible for him to obtain large sums of money as soon as possible.

The personal support was the easiest. The murder of Edward V and Prince Richard had touched the hearts of Englishmen of all classes and had made King Richard III a deeply hated man. London—and, in fact, all of England—was ready to welcome as a hero the man who had defeated and slain the tyrant. As a result, Henry Tudor's entrance into London after the battle was a joyous affair, with the crowds hailing him as their hero and deliverer.

For a great many years, there was a strange misunderstanding about Richmond's joyful reception as he came into the city of London. The original account was written in Latin. Bernard Andreas, the historian who wrote it in 1485, recorded that Henry VII entered the city gates of London "joyfully" (*laetanter*, in Latin). About forty years later, John Speed, one of the first historians describing the event in English, misread the Latin word as *latenter*, which means "secretly," so he assumed that the conqueror had entered the city in a carriage, closed and curtained so he would not be recognized. Other historians followed this man's lead, so for well over a century people believed that Henry had come sneaking into the city in a closed carriage or a curtained litter, which was as far from the truth as it could be. Not until 1902 did James Gairdner, an English historian, go back to the original Latin and discover the mistake. After nearly four centuries, the public was at last treated to a much pleasanter description of the affair.

Henry VII, Tudor King of England from 1485 to 1509. (Portrait, 1505, by an unknown artist)

Henry would have liked his coronation to have taken place soon after his victory at Bosworth Field and his reception in London, but this was not possible. There was a sudden outbreak of a dread disease, the "sweating sickness" (miliary fever), which killed thousands of Londoners and made it completely unsafe for people to gather in crowds. It was necessary to wait until the epidemic was over, and this did not occur until the arrival of cold weather in the fall. Finally, on October 30, 1485, the Archbishop of Canterbury placed the crown on the head of the impatient man and made him, legally and completely, King Henry VII of England.

There still remained the two other types of support to be gained before King Henry could relax and regard the crown as safely his.

In the castle of Sheriff Hutton of Yorkshire were two very important political prisoners. One was Edward Plantagenet, Earl of Warwick, son of Duke George of Clarence, who had died only a few years before. Warwick was felt to be extremely dangerous, for he had been selected by King Richard III as the member of the House of York who should follow him on the throne. King Henry had this rival moved to the Tower of London, and imprisoned there. The other prisoner of Sheriff Hutton was the charming Princess Elizabeth of York. Unlike her relative the earl, she did not go to the Tower but was given honorable escort to her mother's house in London. There was good reason for the new king's consideration. Her line of descent from King Edward III was much more direct than his, and she was a most important member of the House of York. Soon he called upon her and asked her to be his queen. She consented, and they were married on January 18, 1486.

King Henry's claim to the throne was now much more secure. His most dangerous rival was locked in the Tower, and his marriage to Princess Elizabeth guaranteed that there would be no renewal of the Wars of the Roses between the two great royal houses. He was a member of the House of Lancaster; she was a member of the House of York. Whatever descendants they had would belong to both houses. As a further benefit, his new queen was a saintly woman—charming, considerate, and thoughtful. History has quite rightly given her the name of Queen Elizabeth the Good.

Though Henry had established dynastic support, there still remained the problem of financial support.

The surest way for a king to raise money in King Henry's time was by confiscating the estates of wealthy men who had committed treason or other serious crimes. Whom could he charge and with what crime could he charge them? True, a dozen or more great and worthy English noblemen had fought against him at Bosworth Field on August 22, but that was hardly a crime. They were fighting on the side of their lawful king against a little-known earl who had no recognizable claim to the throne. Until King Richard died and Henry Tudor took the crown, these men had done nothing wrong, and as soon as Richard died they had ceased all actions against the victorious earl.

The solution involved a good bit of cleverness and even more dishonesty. Somehow, it must be legally established that Henry had been the rightful king since before the Battle of Bosworth Field. Parliament was the only body which could do this and give it the force of law. Pressure was put on the members of Parliament to record the beginning of Henry's kingship as August 21, 1485, instead of August 22.

The difference made by the one day was enormous. Now it could legally be proved that for an entire day the noblemen who had sided with King Richard III had been fighting against their lawful king, Henry VII. August 22, the day of Bosworth Field, became a day of monstrous treason. It made no sense at all, but by act of Parliament it was made unbeatable law. King Henry had charges brought against the late King Richard, the Duke of Norfolk, the Earl of Surrey, Lords Lovell and Ferrers and many others, stating that "on the 21st. day of August, the first year of the reign of our sovereign lord, they assembled to them a great host, traitorously intending, imagining, and conspiring the destruction of the King's royal person. . . ." The verdict was, of course, guilty, and the lords against whom the charges had been brought were stripped of their titles, their homes and lands, and all possessions. Even those already dead were so stripped, their heirs losing all claims to what they had expected to inherit. Using this dishonest procedure, King Henry was able to build up his possessions until, by the time of his death, he had become the richest monarch in the world.

Another step—a most important one—remained to be taken in securing the safety of the realm. For well over one hundred years, a few men had known about gunpowder—"devil's dust," as Shakespeare would call it in a later day. No one knows who had invented it; some say the Chinese, some the Arabs, and a few an English monk named Roger Bacon. For a long time, no one seems to have realized its real possibilities. Then, in 1453—just four years before the birth of King Henry VII—the Sultan Mohammed II attacked the great city of Constantinople. Among the sultan's weapons were some strange tubes, in which gunpowder could be exploded and used to throw heavy rocks. Gaps were smashed in the walls of Constantinople, the city fell, and the world had acquired a new and very effective weapon, the cannon. Soon smaller firearms appeared—muskets, which could be carried and fired by a single soldier, called a musketeer.

As soon as he came to power, King Henry made certain that he had under his control all the cannons within his realm. Before this time, it had not been difficult to revolt against the government. A group of noblemen could lead out their knights and bowmen with a good chance of defeating the king's knights and bowmen. If the king had artillery, though, and they did not, their chances were poor indeed. Their armored knights and their bowmen could be slaughtered from a distance, and their castles destroyed. With the batteries of artillery in his own hands and a few companies of musketeers organized, the king had much less to fear from revolts.

Still, King Henry did not want to take any chances. He had heard that the inhabitants of the northern part of England, centering on the city of York, were still very much in favor of a king from the York family, instead of a Lancastrian who happened to be married to a York princess. Even more important was the news that three of the nobles who had sided with King Richard—Lord Lovell, Lord Humphrey Stafford, and Thomas Stafford—were raising armies in this northerly area with the thought of renewing the war. A bold move into the north seemed called for.

One would have thought that a king, so menaced by civil war, would have advanced into the rebellious territory at the head of a great army. Instead of an army, King Henry went almost alone, accompanied only by the usual attendants of a royal "progress," or journey. One might have expected that he would take Queen Elizabeth with him, since she was a member of the York family and was popular in the northern region. Instead, he left her at home; he wanted to show that he was not dependent on his queen for retention of his crown, and he did not wish to risk her health, since she was already pregnant with the first of their royal children.

The royal progress worked out precisely as the king had hoped. As he neared the forces of the three hostile nobles, he added to his army about three thousand local men for use if he needed them, but he placed his main dependence on the secret weapon of pardon. Heralds went on ahead, proclaiming complete pardon for all who would submit without fighting. Lord Lovell, fearful that his men would accept the offer, fled and eventually made his way safely to Flanders. The two Staffords also abandoned their men and tried to escape, but they were captured. Lord Humphrey, the elder of the two and the leader, was executed. Thomas was pardoned, as were all of their men who submitted, as most of them did.

With resistance out of the way, King Henry VII continued his triumphal journey in peace through the northern lands. He was enthusiastically received in York and in the other towns and cities which he visited.

From north of the border, King James III of Scotland had been watching King Henry's "progress" and had been much impressed. Soon after the English king returned to London, a Scottish delegation called upon him, offering to renew the treaty of friendship between the English and Scottish governments. The old treaty had lapsed when King Richard III had been killed. The new agreement was duly signed, to the benefit of both countries, and an understanding was reached that King James III, whose queen had recently died, would marry Dowager Queen Elizabeth, the widow of King Edward IV of England. It was further agreed that at some later time two of King James's sons would marry two of dowager Queen Elizabeth's daughters.

As a matter of fact, the marriage agreement with King James III was never carried out, for a group of nobles revolted against the Scottish king in 1488, and his country was split by civil war. The king's oldest son, Prince James, was on the side of the nobles, against his father. In a battle fought at Canglor in June 1488, King James was defeated, and as he fled from the field his horse fell, pinning him down. As King James lay helpless on the ground, he was killed by a soldier disguised as a priest. His son succeeded him on the throne, under the name of King James IV. Like his father, he maintained friendly relations with his English neighbors.

On September 20, 1486—soon after the northern expedition and the Scottish conference but some time before the revolt in Scotland—King Henry's wife, Elizabeth the Good, gave birth to her first child, a son. From the very beginning of his life he was small and weak, for he had been born a month before he was due. Nevertheless, he was a living prince and an heir to the throne. King Henry promptly named him Arthur, hoping to promote the idea that the Tudor family was directly descended from the famous King Arthur of old, who was believed to have presided over the Knights of the Round Table, nearly a thousand years before.

The birth of Prince Arthur gave a look of permanence to the royal family of Tudor and stirred King Henry's enemies into a very strange series of maneuvers, centering on a fifteen-year-old boy, Edward Plantagenet, Earl of Warwick. Before his own fall, King Richard III had named this boy as his chosen successor on the throne, a fact that made him a dangerous rival for King Henry VII and newborn Prince Arthur. He was, at this time, safely lodged as a prisoner in the Tower.

The first step in the plot against the king was to circulate a rumor that young Warwick had died in the Tower. This brought back memories of the two little princes who had been murdered there and tended to arouse dislike for Henry VII. Shortly thereafter, a priest appeared in Dublin, accompanied by an attractive fifteen-year-old boy, who was introduced as Edward Plantagenet, Earl of Warwick. An exciting and totally false story was told of the boy's escape just in time to avoid the fate of his two young relatives, a few years before. Many influential people were deceived by this hoax and pledged allegiance to this supposed Earl of Warwick, rival claimant to the throne. Actually, the boy was the son of an Oxford workman. His real name was Lambert Simnel. He had been carefully trained to play his part to perfection.

King Henry tried in vain to counter the hoax by means of ridicule. He briefly released the real Earl of Warwick from the Tower and made it possible for him to talk to large numbers of interested people, who recognized him and thus knew that the boy in Ireland was an impostor. In the end, though, force had to be used, for Henry's old enemy Lord Lovell brought two thousand trained soldiers from Flanders to support the boy. These men, combined with forces raised in Ireland, invaded England and began an advance through York. They were met at Stoke by the king's heavy cavalry and were slaughtered. Lord Lovell escaped, but many years later his skeleton was found in a secret underground room in a house he owned nearby. Apparently, he had hidden there and had died, either of starvation or of exposure. The priest and the boy surrendered. The priest died in prison, but Lambert Simnel was treated more kindly. He was pardoned and was given work as a scullion in the royal kitchen. Years later, after long and faithful service, he was promoted to the post of royal falconer.

During the first year and a half of his marriage, King Henry VII had been something less than kind to his wife, Queen Elizabeth the Good. Gradually, he realized that he might encounter less trouble in York and other northern lands of his kingdom if he would show more consideration in his treatment of the House of York, of which his queen was now the outstanding member. For one thing, he had been crowned but she had not. On November 25, 1487, the ceremony was performed. Clad in "white cloth of gold of damask, with a mantle furred with ermine," wearing on her head a circle of gold ornamented with precious stones, with her fair yellow hair hanging plain behind her back, she was borne through London reclining on a litter, shaded from the sun by a canopy of cloth of gold, carried by four knights of the Order of the Bath. Following the coronation, she dined with two noblewomen sitting at her feet under the table while two others knelt beside her to offer a napkin when desired. It is said that King Henry watched the ceremony from behind a lattice, and that never after that day did he show her the lack of regard that had characterized the first two years of their marriage.

One of the persistent worries of the early years of King Henry's reign was the power which had gradually been accumulated by some of the great English noblemen. To control it, he had Parliament pass two important laws. One forbade a growing practice called maintenance, which consisted of the building up of private followings—almost small armies. Members of such groups wore their noble's livery, or uniform, and were well armed. With the aid of the protective walls of the private castles, they could make it impossible for a sheriff or other local lawman to enforce the laws or even the king's orders. They also provided ready-made armed bands for possible use by anyone wishing to revolt against King Henry's government. When the maintenance of such private forces was done away with, King Henry VII felt more secure.

Even when a powerful, lawbreaking noble had been arrested and brought to justice, it was still difficult to punish him. The power and influence of such a man was usually too great to make it safe for the members of a regular court to try him and sentence him. To correct this, King Henry had Parliament create a new and stronger court. The members of the court were themselves powerful nobles, so they had less to fear from the men they tried. They were also given added powers, not granted to the lesser courts. For example, they were permitted to torture witnesses and defenders in order to force them to give desired testimony, and they could give a rather wide variety of punishments for an equally wide variety of charges, though they were not permitted to assign the death penalty. Because its first meeting was held in a room with a star-decorated ceiling, this feared and hated new court came to be known as the Court of the Star Chamber. Even today, centuries after that court has ceased to exist, secret, irregular, or slanted legal moves are still spoken of as star-chamber procedures.

The reign of King Henry VII was more greedy than warlike. He dearly loved to pile up wealth, but he hated to spend any of it. He was far more at home in his countinghouse than in a military camp, happier in his gown and felt slippers than in a suit of armor, more comfortable upon an upholstered chair than on a horse. No war was likely to interest him that did not promise a good chance of financial profit.

South of England, across the English Channel, lay the Duchy of Brittany, now a part of France but then largely independent under the rule of elderly Duke Francis. King Charles VIII of France wanted Brittany and declared war against the duke to get it. Henry was much indebted to Duke Francis, who had taken him in and sheltered him during the reign of Richard III, when Henry had been a fugitive from England. Instead of coming to the duke's aid, though, he engaged in dickering and managed to keep the situation unsettled until the end of 1488, when Duke Francis was dead and the French had occupied most of the duchy.

The duke had a daughter named Anne, who tried to carry on the war after her father's death. One of her methods was to put pressure directly on King Henry to repay his debt of honor. When he could no longer ignore the matter, he promised to send Princess Anne an English army of six thousand bowmen. At the same time, he compelled Parliament to pay him 75,000 pounds to support the army.

The bowmen were sent to Brittany, but, as he sent them, King Henry VII announced that they would stay there only half a year and would fight only in self-defense. As a result, they did not have to fight at all, for the French avoided them while conquering the duchy, and they avoided the French. At the end of the six months, they returned home. King Henry had not used up all of the 75,000 pounds and what had not been used, he kept for himself. Parliament, having voted the money, placed added taxes on the people to raise it, thus causing futile riots in the northern counties of England.

Brittany had now lost its independence, and Princess Anne had been forced to give her duchy permanently to France by agreeing to marry King Charles VIII, whom she detested. At this point, King Henry sent another English army across the channel, announcing that he was going to punish the French king. At the same time, however, he sent word to King Charles that he would bring his army home again and make peace if Charles would pay him 149,000 pounds. Charles agreed, so this army, too, was withdrawn. War, for King Henry VII, involved few victories and little fighting but yielded some rather spectacular profits.

As if one impostor were not enough, King Henry VII suffered from the pretensions of two others during the general period of his little "war" with France. The first of these presented even more of a threat than had Lambert Simnel, some years before.

This impostor first came to public notice when he landed at Cork, Ireland, from a vessel which had sailed from Lisbon, Portugal. He was about twenty years old, handsome, well spoken, and very familiar with even the most minor details of the events, places, and personalities mentioned in his story. He was, so he claimed, Richard, Duke of York, the younger of the two little princes who had been imprisoned and, presumably, murdered in the Tower. No record survives of the manner in which he answered the many difficult questions he must have been asked: How he had managed to escape with his life when King Richard III was having his brother murdered; where he had been living during the years since his escape; what proof he had of the identity he was claiming. He must have handled himself cleverly, for somehow he managed to convince most of his questioners. What is more, he managed to get their support in his campaign to win for himself the crown of England, which, so he maintained, belonged to him and not to Henry Tudor. Among the most influential of the Irish supporters whom the young man gained for his cause were former Mayor O'Water, of the city of Cork, and the Earl of Desmond.

In the midst of King Henry's profitable war with King Charles VIII of France, the young man who called himself Richard, Duke of York, suddenly moved his headquarters from Ireland to France. This was a good location, for the court of King Charles had attracted many influential Englishmen who, for one reason or another, were opposed to King Henry. The new sanctuary did not last long, though, for peace was soon made and the impostor was ordered by King Charles to leave France. He went to Burgundy, where he was made welcome by Dowager Duchess Margaret.

The impostor must have been a very persuasive person, for Duchess Margaret was the aunt of the real Richard, Duke of York—the young man whom he claimed to be. Either she was completely deceived or she decided to play his game for reasons not very evident today. She fondly referred to him as "the White Rose of England" and permitted him to use her court as a gathering place for plotters and as a possible starting point for his planned invasion of England.

Thoroughly alarmed, King Henry VII tried to persuade the Archduke of Burgundy to expel the impostor, but his request was refused. Angered, Henry then cut off all trade between England and Burgundy, and he also withdrew from the Burgundian city of Antwerp an English cloth market that had been adding considerably to the wealth of the little European duchy. At the same time, he sent some trusted Englishmen to the duchess's court to see what they could learn of the conspiracy.

King Henry's spies did well. By pretending to be enemies of their king, they gained the confidence of the impostor. They learned that his real name was Perkin Warbeck. As a native of Burgundy, he had learned the English language and much English history by associating with English merchants in his native country. The spies also learned and reported the names of a number of trusted English noblemen who had been giving aid and encouragement to the false Duke of York. A number of these were promptly arrested, and three were put to death.

Among those charged with minor participation in the plot was Lord Clifford. Falling to his knees, he begged the king to forgive him, and the king at last agreed, provided Clifford would supply some useful evidence. In fulfilling this requirement, Clifford uttered a name which King Henry would much rather not have heard—that of Sir William Stanley. At first, the king refused to believe that Sir William could have had any part in this wicked plot against his throne. It was Sir William Stanley who had come to his rescue at Bosworth Field when he was in danger of being killed, and it was this same man who had picked up the crown of Richard III and handed it to him. Sir William Stanley had served him well. Still, Sir William was a very wealthy man, with broad lands and valuable possessions which would become the king's if Stanley were convicted and punished. The execution was permitted to take place without further question.

Perkin Warbeck had not been captured, and he was not yet through. From Flanders, he led a small force by sea to the English port of Deal, but he was driven away with the loss of 169 of his followers, some killed, some captured. It made little difference which, for King Henry sent word that all of those captured should be hanged, and they were. Joined by another force under the Earl of Desmond, the impostor now sailed to Ireland and laid siege to Waterford. Again he was beaten, fleeing after he had lost three of his ships. Some time later, he took refuge in Scotland, where King James IV befriended him and permitted him to marry a Scottish noblewoman, a near relative of the king himself. Encouraged by this, Warbeck tried another invasion of England, supported by some of James's Scottish troops. He found, though, that Englishmen no longer would help his cause, and he was repulsed, captured, and confined in the Tower.

In the meantime, the third impostor had made an appearance. His name was Ralph Wilford, but he maintained that he was really the Earl of Warwick, whom Lambert Simnel had earlier impersonated. Wilford was arrested, and he and Perkin Warbeck were both accused of treason and executed.

The real Earl of Warwick became the innocent victim of this ridiculous series of masquerades. Though he had long been a prisoner in the Tower and thus presumably safely insulated from either the temptation or the opportunity to do anything harmful to the reigning family, he was nevertheless accused of treason. His real "crime" was his ancestry, for he was the last surviving member of the Plantagenet family with a valid claim to King Henry's throne. It was barely conceivable that at some time in the future he might become a genuine menace to the House of Tudor. Two men had already caused trouble by pretending to be he. Word of these impostors had spread abroad and was already beginning to make it more difficult for King Henry to arrange a suitable marriage contract for his frail young son, Prince Arthur. In particular, King Ferdinand and Queen Isabella of Spain were expressing reluctance to permit their daughter, Princess Catherine of Aragon, to marry into a family line which might be overturned. The unfortunate Earl of Warwick was found guilty of treason and was put to death.

In 1489, when Prince Arthur was less than three years old, King Henry VII and Queen Elizabeth the Good had a second child. It was a girl, a princess who received the name of Margaret. Considering the delicate state of Arthur's health, a sound, strong son would have been most desirable, but a daughter would be of little use. Should anything happen to her brother, she could never reign. There had never been a reigning Queen of England, and presumably there never would be.

Since King Henry VII was rightly known as the builder of a great fortune, it is worth while to look at some of the methods used to increase his income. By far the most important method was the creation of a steady income through taxation.

Very early in his reign, the king was granted by Parliament the proceeds from certain taxes known as tonnage and poundage. These were taxes of so much a ton on the cargoes of ships entering English ports and so much a pound on goods sold locally. Earlier kings had enjoyed such receipts, so the people were accustomed to them, and there was not much protest. Later, wanting more money, the king twice tried to lay taxes directly on the poorer classes. This caused such widespread resistance that King Henry and his advisors decided against trying it a third time. Some other form of taxation must be found.

The answer lay in what were supposed to be direct, voluntary gifts to the king from wealthy men. They were called benevolences. Actually, they were not voluntary at all. The donors were approached by the king's collectors, who not only told them that they were expected to give gifts to the king but also told them how much to give. Those who refused to give soon found themselves ruined by government pressure on their sources of income.

Most famous of the king's collectors was Bishop Morton, who had invented a method of persuasion known as "Morton's fork." Men who lived richly and spent freely were made to give large gifts because they so obviously were wealthy, and those who lived simply were made to contribute heavily because their inexpensive way of life must have left so much money available. Either way, there was no escape. When once the promises had been made, hard-bitten collectors forced payment in harsh ways. The most hated collectors were Richard Empson and Edmund Dudley.

Although one of the most miserly and penny-pinching of monarchs, King Henry VII did sometimes open his purse for a worthy cause. There lived in Bristol, England, an experienced Italian sea captain named John Cabot, who had developed a theory that it would be easier and quicker to reach the seaports of Asia by sailing westward around the world than by passing south around Africa and then sailing northeastward, as was then being done. Cabot did not know how large the world really is, nor did he know that North and South America lay west of Europe and blocked the western route to Asia.

In 1493, word reached England that another Italian navigator, Christopher Columbus, had had the same idea and had beaten Cabot in discovering the western route. King Ferdinand and Queen Isabella of Spain had put up the money for the voyage, which had reached some islands that Columbus believed lay off the coast of Asia. Actually, the islands that had been discovered and claimed for Spain were parts of the Bahama and West Indies groups, lying off the southeastern coast of North America.

Excited by the apparent success of Columbus's voyage, and not wishing the Spanish rulers to draw ahead of him in a profitable venture, King Henry supplied a ship for Cabot and gave him permission to lead an English expedition westward. In June 1497, the ship reached Cape Breton Island, at the mouth of the St. Lawrence River. The next year, with two ships, Cabot found the coast of Greenland, then sailed along the North American coast as far south as Virginia, claiming the land for England as he went. He, too, was puzzled by the fact that he could find no trace of the great and ancient civilizations of Asia, for he still believed that that was the continent he had reached.

The same comment can fairly be made about each of the great explorers: "Before he set out, he did not know where he was going; when he arrived, he did not know where he was; and, when he returned, he did not know where he had been."

# 2
# PRINCE HENRY

THE third child born to King Henry VII and Queen Elizabeth the Good provided a refreshing contrast to the two who had come before. Unlike sister Margaret, he was a male. Unlike brother Arthur, he was healthy —a big, strong, full-term baby boy. He was given the name of Henry and assigned to the care of an ample nurse named Anne Luke.

Prince Henry was a precocious child, but no amount of precocity could possibly have prepared him for the titles and responsibilities that were presently thrust upon him. In April 1493 —when he was less than two years old—he appeared in public, clasped in Anne Luke's arms, and was officially assigned his first two offices of state: Constable of Dover Castle and Warden of the Cinque Ports. In the months that followed, other titles and honors were bestowed: Duke of York, Earl Marshal, Warden of the Scottish Marches, and member of the Order of the Garter and the Order of the Bath, the latter including the strapping of a spur to the baby heel! Brother Arthur already had a similar list of titles and offices, perhaps even more imposing.

At first glance, it seems ridiculous that such exalted positions should be bestowed on two little boys, both far too young to understand the responsibilities or perform the duties. King Henry VII, though, was thinking of money. Each office provided a fine income for the person who occupied the honorary top position.

The actual work would be done by underlings, the deputy officials. How much better it was to have the money coming in to members of the royal family—into the possession of King Henry VII—than into the possession of some unrelated nobleman who might or might not remain loyal to his king!

Since Arthur, as Prince of Wales, was to follow his father on the throne, some other worthy career had to be found for little Henry. Next to royal rule, the Church seemed to offer the best possibilities. King Henry decided that his young namesake must be trained for holy orders, with the eventual post of Archbishop of Canterbury in mind. This was the highest office in the entire Roman Catholic Church in England.

John Skelton, Prince Henry's tutor from 1496 until 1502—from the age of five to eleven—must have exercised a great influence upon his mind. Skelton was studying for the priesthood; he was a widely educated man; he was renowned as a poet; and he had a knowledge of history surpassed by very few. What Lady Margaret Beaufort, the prince's grandmother who selected Skelton, may not have known, was his cynical questioning of the teachings of the Church, which would eventually cause his expulsion from his rectorship; his irreverent views concerning some of the most highly regarded people of England's past and present; his tendency to intersperse shocking and scandalous writings among his loftier pieces of poetry and prose; and his reckless habit of uttering and writing bitter satire about everyone and everything that displeased him.

One book Skelton wrote was beyond reproach. It was entitled *Speculum Principis* (*A Mirror for Princes*) and was written specifically for Prince Henry's guidance. It contained much good advice, most of which his pupil never bothered to follow. Especially, "Choose a wife for yourself. Prize her always and uniquely." Though the first part of this admonition was to be followed not once but half a dozen times, the latter part was consistently ignored.

The most amazing accomplishment of John Skelton was his success in living to the age of sixty-nine and dying a natural death. Few people in his time managed to live nearly that long even when exercising the greatest of care, and John Skelton was anything but careful. Three of his most vicious satires—*Colin Clout, Speak Parrot,* and *Why Come Ye not to Court?*—were aimed directly at King Henry's minister Thomas Wolsey, then one of the most powerful men in the kingdom. This was a time when even the mildest of written or expressed criticism might well be the cause of arrest and execution, but Skelton's actions were overlooked. Some years later, when his former pupil was King of England, Skelton received the rewards and honors of the office of Poet Laureate of England, which indicates that whatever he had taught the little boy had been understood, appreciated, and judged to be good.

Although a good deal of credit for Prince Henry's rapid progress toward an excellent education must go to Skelton and to the tutors who followed him, one must recognize that these men were dealing with an exceptional pupil. Henry learned easily and rapidly, for he had an excellent memory, an active mind, and a real desire to learn anything that seemed likely to be of value to him. In addition, he had a rich, resonant voice, a love of music, and a talent for mastering instruments. His strong, well-coordinated body not only added sharpness to his mental processes but also aided greatly in his mastery of such other princely pursuits as riding, hunting, and the use of weapons. Prince Arthur's education was similar. He also had a good mind, but he had neither the good health nor the strength of body to match Henry's accomplishments.

In Prince Henry's day, the children of royal families had little to say about the choosing of husbands or wives for themselves. Royal children were valuable possessions of their families, who were engaged in a constant game of finding them mates who would bring important alliances, trade treaties, and financial help to the home governments. One's personal feelings did not matter. If the marriage would help the kingdom, it was likely to take place. If not, it didn't.

King Henry VII was no exception when it came to using his children as pawns in the game of international relations. As early as 1492, when Prince Arthur was only five years old, his father signed a marriage treaty with the Spanish monarchs—Ferdinand of Aragon and Isabella of Castile—pledging Arthur as the husband of the Spanish Princess Catherine of Aragon, who was about ten months older than Arthur. As Ferdinand and Isabella had just undertaken the financing of Christopher Columbus's explorations, they were unwilling to promise a large dowry for their daughter. Four years later, though, a new treaty was signed, greatly increasing the amount.

Prince Arthur and Princess Catherine were officially married on May 19, 1501, in a ceremony held in one of the English manor houses. The fifteen-year-old-bride was not even present at her wedding, for her parents felt that she was not yet quite old enough for married life. She was kept at home in Spain, while the Spanish ambassador represented her in the ceremony. Five months later, though, when Prince Arthur had had his fifteenth birthday, King Henry VII demanded that she come to England, and her parents reluctantly sent her. A second wedding ceremony was planned before the prince and princess could begin living as man and wife. This time, the bride intended to be present.

Word of the landing of Princess Catherine at Plymouth was accompanied by a further message which caused King Henry VII great uneasiness. She was not to be seen by him or by Prince Arthur until the marriage ceremony. Wishing to see for himself whether there was anything wrong with her, he summoned Prince Arthur and had attendants, guards, and horses assembled. Then father and son, leading the cavalcade, set out to the south to meet the oncoming bride.

They found Princess Catherine at the stately mansion of the

Bishop of Bath, at Dogmersfield, where she and her attendants had arrived shaken by a long, rough voyage from Spain and soaked by a heavy English rainstorm. The princess had scarcely bathed and changed from her damp and travel-stained clothes into more comfortable attire when there was a sudden disturbance in the lower hallway. King Henry and the prince were there, demanding to see Princess Catherine. Her attendants objected, but the king shouted to his translator: "You may inform the lords that the King of England will see the Princess, even if she is already in her bed!"

Into the room strode a group of men led by King Henry VII and Prince Arthur. As the princess arose from her chair to greet them, King Henry was very much relieved to see that his fears had been groundless. There was nothing wrong with the princess. King Ferdinand and Queen Isabella were giving full value in the bargain.

Communication, though, was difficult. King Henry and Prince Arthur spoke only two languages, English and French. The princess knew only Spanish. For a few minutes, there was confusion and misunderstanding. Then—almost miraculously, it seemed—a method developed, awkward and halting but quite useable. The Bishop of Bath knew English and Latin. A priest in the princess's train of followers knew Latin and Spanish. A question might go from English to Latin to Spanish, and its answer from Spanish to Latin to English. Little by little, the reserve thawed away, and as it did the prince and princess experienced a growing attraction for one another. Hand clutched in hand, they replighted their vows—joyfully, this time.

With all anxiety removed, joy and merrymaking took over. The princess summoned her minstrels, her musicians, and her court jester, and until well into the evening a most enjoyable time was had by all. Toward the end, Catherine even overcame her modesty sufficiently to demonstrate some graceful Spanish dance steps. As they parted, the prince and princess exchanged a kiss as a symbol of their warm regard for one another and of their pledge of marriage.

Two happy surprises awaited Princess Catherine upon her arrival at the English royal palace at Greenwich. One was Queen Elizabeth, wife of King Henry VII and mother of Prince Arthur. Though the queen spoke no Spanish and Catherine, as yet, spoke no English, the two quickly became dear friends. Having been a member of the rival House of York, the queen could imagine all too well the problems and embarrassments faced by a young princess marrying into a foreign royal family.

The other surprise was Prince Henry, Arthur's younger brother. It was hard to believe that this large, strong, and energetic young man was only ten years old—five years younger than his brother and nearly six years younger than she. Squiring her around, as he did during the weeks before her marriage to his brother, he displayed an almost adult self-confidence, in sharp contrast to Arthur's timid diffidence. In contests which they attended together he delighted in showing his prospective sister-in-law his skill with sword, javelin, and bow, and his prowess as a mounted knight, jousting in the lists, clad in a complete suit of armor which had been made especially for him.

On November 19, 1501, Prince Arthur and Princess Catherine were married in a beautiful and impressive ceremony in St. Paul's Cathedral.

It was to be a short marriage. Less than a month after the ceremony, King Henry VII sent his son Arthur to Wales, to learn at first hand the problems facing an administrator in the wild outlands of the kingdom. Catherine accompanied him. Suddenly, after four months in Wales, the heir to the throne collapsed, stricken by a deadly illness, the exact nature of which is not now known. He died on April 2, 1502.

The prince's death raised some serious problems. The heir to the throne was gone. Two other children, Princess Elisabeth and Prince Edmund, had died in early childhood. Prince Henry was being raised and educated for a career in the Church. True, two daughters were alive and well—Princess Margaret, now thirteen, and Princess Mary, six—but no queen had ever reigned in England. Prince Henry would have to give up all thoughts of a Church career, all plans for becoming Archbishop of Canterbury, and prepare instead to occupy the throne of England. Only thus could the Tudor line, which his father had planted on the throne, continue to reign.

There was also the question of what should be done with Princess Catherine of Aragon, now a widow at the age of sixteen. The first thought was to send her back to Spain, but neither the Princess nor her father, King Ferdinand, wanted this. It might well mean the cancellation of the promising English-Spanish alliance against the growing power of France, and in any event it would mark the failure of a cherished mission.

No sooner had the sad news of Arthur's death reached Spain than King Ferdinand and Queen Isabella sent a special emissary to the English court to urge and to insist upon an immediate marriage of their daughter to Arthur's younger brother, Henry. King Henry VII, though, was not to be rushed. He answered the Spanish representative by quoting from the Book of Leviticus: ". . . and if a man shall take his brother's wife, it is an unclean thing: he hath uncovered his brother's nakedness; they shall be childless." At the same time, he was carefully studying the European situation, court by court, to see if there might be a more advantageous marriage available for his son.

King Ferdinand and Queen Isabella took a different view. Through their emissary, they maintained that the quotation from Leviticus did not apply because the marriage of Arthur and Catherine had never been consummated, so that she was not truly his widow. The shortness of the marriage, the youthfulness of the bride and groom, and Prince Arthur's delicate state of health were all mentioned, as was the statement of Catherine's duenna, Donna Elvira, who swore that her little mistress was still a virgin. This marriage would be quite all right. All that would be needed would be an appeal to the Pope, who could issue a decree, as he had done when Catherine's sister Maria had married the husband of her late sister Isabella.

King Henry disagreed. In his view, the Pope was the highest officer of the Church, but even he could not set aside the holy law of the Bible. Prince Henry was his one remaining son, his one hope for a continuing Tudor dynasty of kings, and he wished to take no chances with a marriage that might be set to naught by this definite statement in Leviticus.

The matter remained unsettled, while Princess Catherine lived from one unhappy day to the next and while Prince Henry's father continued to survey the courts of Europe for a better arrangement for his son.

Queen Elizabeth the Good did not long outlive Prince Arthur. About the time of his death, she became pregnant with her seventh and last child. The baby—a girl named Catherine—was born, but the mother did not recover from the strain of childbirth. She died on February 11, 1503—her thirty-seventh birthday—and the newborn princess followed her a few days later.

Even the death of his beloved wife could not keep King Henry VII from laying plans for his own betterment. A new wife could bring him consolation and—if properly chosen—a good deal of money. The parents of Princess Catherine of Aragon had already paid an installment of 100,000 crowns toward her dowry, and there was another 100,000 still unpaid. If he, himself, should marry the girl, he would not have to return the first installment and could demand the payment of the second. A message was at once dispatched to Spain including the suggestion.

King Ferdinand and Queen Isabella were horrified. It would

be far better for Princess Catherine to marry Prince Henry. If this could not be done, they demanded that she return to Spain, bringing the first installment of the dowry.

Faced with the loss of 100,000 crowns, King Henry yielded. On his twelfth birthday, Prince Henry was formally betrothed to seventeen-year-old Princess Catherine. The wedding itself was to take place three years later, by which time King Ferdinand and Queen Isabella would have paid the second installment of the dowry.

King Henry VII also played a part in the marriage of his daughter Margaret, who became the bride of James IV of Scotland in an important ceremony which would eventually bring about the union of England and Scotland under a single government.

King Henry had, as yet, not found a new mate of his own. The late King of Naples, it seemed, had willed his widow an immense fortune. King Henry opened negotiations for the lady's hand, but quickly broke them off when he learned that the new King of Naples had refused to let the lady inherit her riches.

Late the next year, 1504, Queen Isabella of Castile, died, leaving her kingdom to her daughter Juana and to Juana's husband, Archduke Philip the Handsome, Governor of the Netherlands. King Ferdinand retained his own kingdom of Aragon and some rights as an administrator of Castile until his daughter could take over.

Early in 1506, Juana and Philip left the Netherlands for Spain, but bad weather forced their ship into the English harbor of Falmouth. There, they made the serious mistake of going ashore without official permission. They were politely but firmly arrested and compelled to visit King Henry in his castle. Before they were released, after some three months of enforced hospitality, they had had to agree to a marriage between Philip's sister, Margaret of Savoy, and King Henry, with Philip putting up a dowry of 300,000 crowns; to a marriage between Philip's son

Charles and King Henry's daughter Princess Mary; to a commercial treaty that favored English merchants over those of Flanders; and to surrender the Earl of Suffolk, an enemy of King Henry's who had found refuge in the Netherlands. For his part, King Henry had agreed not to execute the Earl of Suffolk and had lent Duke Philip some money to be used in the continuation of his voyage.

Not long afterward, news was received that considerably changed King Henry's plans for gaining a wife. Archduke Philip the Handsome had died, leaving Juana a widow. She would be a far better wife than Margaret of Savoy, being richer, more attractive, and a queen. She was also young enough to bear children, and this could be important to a king trying to strengthen his royal line. Immediate word was sent to King Ferdinand of Aragon, asking his help and cooperation. Catherine of Aragon, who had been kept in near-poverty by King Henry, was also enlisted in the campaign to gain her father's help.

King Ferdinand of Aragon was in no mood to cooperate. The shock of her husband's death had driven Juana insane. She had had her husband's body embalmed and placed in a glass coffin and was traveling about Spain with it. King Ferdinand felt that his interests would be better served by having his daughter declared incompetent and placed in his charge than by having her marry King Henry VII. He wanted control of Castile placed permanently in his own hands. Though King Henry said that he would be happy to marry "Juana the Mad," since she was still young enough to bear children, his suit was rejected.

There would be no other queen for King Henry VII. He had always been frail, and in his later years had suffered increasingly from gout. On April 21, 1509, he died quietly in his bed. Kneeling at the bedside, deep in prayer, was handsome and athletic Prince Henry, who would now follow his father on the throne as King Henry VIII of England.

# 3
# THE NEW YOUNG KING

SELDOM has there been a greater contrast between successive monarchs than that between quiet, secretive, miserly old King Henry VII and handsome, young, athletic, free-spending King Henry VIII, whose hand seized the wheel of state as his father's dead hand dropped away from it.

As the news spread throughout England, there was a quickening of the senses like that which comes with the first warm days of spring. Things would be different, now! The new king was saying that there would be less taxing and more spending. Throughout England—first in London, then in the outlying towns —mobs seized and abused the tax men, then threw them into cells to await more formal punishment. Chief among those taken were old King Henry's two top tax advisors, Richard Empson and Edmund Dudley.

Most of the reaction to the new regime was cheerful, rather than bitter. Almost at once, more modish costumes in brighter colors began to appear. Painting and sculpture seemed to take on new life. The general feeling was one of holiday relaxation after a long and boring period of uninspired labor.

The royal court was the center and the pacesetter for the new liveliness. After years of guidance and direction, King Henry VIII was now free to do what he wished at court.

It is a bit misleading to speak of "the court" as though it were a place where the king was to be found. Actually, the court consisted of people—of the king and of the officials, advisors, friends, and associates who surrounded him. Nor was the court always to be found at any one place. Henry had inherited eight great homes, or castles, from his father, and in the course of his reign he would add eight more. In his early years as king, the greatest part of his time was spent at Greenwich Palace, beside the Thames River, about five miles downstream from London Tower. It is thought that his great interest in the building up of England's navy stemmed from watching the great warships which often lay at anchor in the Thames opposite Greenwich Palace.

Because of his original training for the Church, Henry had received far less training for the kingship than would have been the case if he had been the intended heir to the throne from the beginning of his life. As a result, he felt himself unprepared in his early years and tended to leave the running of the government to those who had grown accustomed to it during his father's reign. For a time, the new king's grandmother, Margaret, Countess of Richmond, remained in charge of appointments, handling continuation of service into the new regime. William Warham, Archbishop of Canterbury, continued on as Lord Chancellor; Richard Fox, Bishop of Winchester, as Lord Privy Seal; Thomas Ruthal, Bishop of Durham, as Royal Secretary; and Thomas Howard, Earl of Surrey, as Lord Treasurer. These and others ensured a smooth continuation of the day-to-day business of government while the new, young king, still not quite eighteen years of age, enjoyed himself and prepared to play a part in governing some time in the future.

Now and then, during this early, carefree period, King Henry would make a decision that would cause his courtiers to realize that his mind was capable of something more serious than the round of pleasures which seemed to occupy so much of his life. Once, for example, a representative of King Louis XII of France appeared in court bearing a letter which someone had sent out over King Henry's signature, requesting an extension of Henry VII's peace treaty with France. King Henry read the letter with growing irritation, then shouted out, "Who wrote this letter? In it, I ask peace of the King of France, who dare not look at me, let alone make war!" To those present, this was a strong indication that before long King Henry VIII would be doing far more governing than he had done up to that time.

Perhaps even more to the point was King Henry's treatment of Empson and Dudley, his father's grasping tax advisors and collectors who had been thrown into prison soon after the old king's death. As the story of their unsavory activities was revealed, King Henry VIII realized that he could increase his own popularity by making good use of the bitter hatred these two men had built up among the people. Whoever punished Empson and Dudley would become a hero to the people! The two were charged with dishonesty and unlawful activities, but they were able to prove that all they had done was to carry out the orders of King Henry VII. This was embarrassing. New charges were brought—wholly imaginary ones this time—that the two had conspired to kidnap Prince Henry when his father died and to seize the throne for themselves. They were found guilty of these ridiculous charges and were beheaded in the Tower.

A king should have a queen, for if his line is to continue on the throne there must be children. Moreover, if the country is sixteenth century England, where no queen had ever reigned, there must be boy children. To King Henry, it seemed that marriage was one of his very early necessities.

Six years before, on his twelfth birthday, he had been formally betrothed to his brother's widow, Catherine of Aragon. Two years later, almost to the day, he had asked that the betrothal be canceled. This had been done, probably to clear the way for the ill-fated attempt by Henry VII to marry the girl himself. Since that time, the Spanish princess had lived an unsettled and lonely life in England, with few comforts and little money. Pride had alone kept her from going back to Spain.

The princess was now almost twenty-four years old, and eighteen-year-old King Henry was finding himself deeply attracted to her. There was also a persistent rumor that the late king, wanting to leave his country secure through a Spanish alliance, had expressed a deathbed wish that Prince Henry marry Princess Catherine. Be that as it may, the new king declared his intention of marrying the princess.

No sooner had the news begun to spread than a bitter quarrel broke out. Pope Julius II in Rome and Archbishop Warham in England were both strongly opposed to the marriage, both quoting the prophecy in Leviticus that if a man shall marry his brother's widow they shall be childless. Others, who favored the marriage, quoted a passage from Deuteronomy urging a man to marry the widow of his deceased brother and produce children. From Spain, King Ferdinand quoted the Princess's duenna, Donna Elvira, who swore that her mistress had never truly been married, for the marriage had not been consummated because of Prince Arthur's poor health. Countering this was the testimony of some of Arthur's friends, who stated that on the morning after the wedding Arthur had called for wine, saying, "Marriage is a thirsty business."

There can be no doubt that King Henry was strongly attracted by Princess Catherine, and the vigor of the opposition merely made him that much more determined to marry her. On June 3, 1509, a quiet, private wedding was held in the Chapel of the Observant Friars in Greenwich. Ordinarily, a royal wedding would have been the occasion for an elaborate and expensive ceremony, but England was still officially in mourning for the late King Henry VII.

Queen Catherine was not unattractive during the early years

of her marriage, having a good figure, regular features, a smooth complexion, and a glory of red-gold hair. She was, moreover, of an ardent disposition, as she was very much in love with King Henry, and he was very much in love with her. On their wedding day, he gave her one of his most cherished treasures, his mother's prayer book, inscribed, "If your remembrance is according to *my* affection, I shall not be forgotten in your prayers, for I am yours, Henry R., for ever."

Besides her devotion to King Henry and to England, Queen Catherine had two other profound loyalties. She was an ardent Roman Catholic, with complete belief in the rightness of the Pope, and she had an undiminished faithfulness to her father's kingdom of Spain. In fact, she regarded herself as King Ferdinand's agent in England. Not long after her marriage to Henry, she included in a letter to her father the statement, "These kingdoms of Your Highness are in great tranquillity," which was indeed an unusual statement to be written by a Queen of England to a King of Spain. This double loyalty, however, did not interfere with her success in learning the English language, quickly and well. Almost from the time of her marriage, English was the language which she customarily used in her daily life.

A famous statesman of the Holy Roman Empire, Mercurio Gattinara, once said, "Princes do not marry for love; they take wives only to beget children." Like most such statements, this one was only partly true. There was love between King Henry and Queen Catherine, but there was also a great necessity for the birth of healthy boys as heirs to the throne. Of the two factors, the necessity for heirs was the more important. From the very day of their wedding, both the king and the queen wanted a baby as quickly as possible—hopefully, a boy, who would be but the first of many.

On June 24, almost three weeks after their wedding, King Henry and Queen Catherine went by boat to the Tower of

Queen Catherine of Aragon in middle age. (Artist unknown)

London, where tradition required that they should spend the night before their coronation. The next day, both were crowned in Westminster Abbey by the Archbishop of Canterbury. On this day, Catherine was dressed in a magnificent gown of white satin and gold. The most significant item of her costume was a filmy white bridal veil—the symbol of virginity—which she wore to indicate that her marriage to Prince Arthur had never been consummated.

Within a matter of weeks, the queen was pregnant. This brought great happiness to the royal pair, but they were doomed to disappointment. In January—three months before the child was due—it was born dead. The fact that it was a girl, and therefore would not have been an heir to the throne, helped the unhappy would-be parents withstand the sorrow and disappointment, and in a letter to King Ferdinand, Catherine wrote, "The King, my lord, took it cheerfully. I thank God for such a husband."

# 4
# FOREIGN RIVALRIES

A<small>MONG</small> the many valuable assets inherited by King Henry VIII from his royal father, few if any were of greater value than an unusual churchman named Thomas Wolsey.

Wolsey's beginnings were humble, but his abilities were immense. He was born in Ipswich, northeast of London, in 1475, the son of a well-to-do butcher. Not wishing to follow his father's occupation, he studied for the priesthood at Magdalen College, Oxford University, and was ordained a priest in 1498. Bishop Fox, who held the office of Lord Privy Seal, early recognized the young clergyman's abilities and steered him into government service. Soon he was performing various minor services directly for King Henry VII. The activity which particularly called the young priest to the king's attention was his adroit handling of King Henry's suit for the hand of Margaret of Savoy, in 1506. It was through no fault of Wolsey's that his clever campaign came to naught when King Henry suddenly changed his mind and began grasping, instead, for the hand of Juana the Mad. Though the king lost both ladies, he was more than a little mollified by the thought that he had gained a very able assistant. By the time of the death of King Henry VII, Wolsey had risen to the very respectable church post of Dean of Lincoln.

It was under King Henry VIII, though, that Thomas Wolsey experienced his meteoric rise to power and wealth. Henry needed help, for his authority as king was seriously limited during these first years of his reign. By the terms of his father's will, he could not act on his own but had to confer with a group of conservative older statesmen, friends of his late father. Typical of the members of the Council, as it was called, were such elderly churchmen as Bishop Warham, Bishop Fox, and Bishop Fisher. In one way or another, all of the members disapproved of their new, young king. Some disapproved of his activities on the athletic and hunting fields, at the jousting barrier, and on the dance floor, saying that his mind should be on more important things and that he should always be present when affairs of state were being discussed. Others agreed with a statement made by one of the Council members: "Let the King hawk and hunt and not intermeddle with old men's cares."

Despite his many competing interests, King Henry did have some serious things he wished to do. What he needed above all else was an experienced elder statesman to champion his chosen causes and help him convince the Council members of their rightness. Thomas Wolsey precisely and efficiently filled this need.

There was a certain irony in the manner in which Wolsey came to play an active part in young King Henry's government. Bishop Fox and Thomas Howard, the Earl of Surrey, were engaged in a struggle for control of the Council. Fox found himself unable to hold his own with Surrey but felt certain that with Wolsey's aid he could do so. Accordingly, he called King Henry's attention to the talented churchman, and presently Wolsey was playing a part in the making of government policy. It did Bishop Fox little good, though, for Thomas Wolsey presently supplanted both Fox and Surrey and, in fact, the Council as a whole. It was not long before he and King Henry, in that order, were, to all intents and purposes, the government of England.

When King Henry VIII came to the throne, the two most

powerful nations on the continent were France, ruled by King Louis XII, and Spain, ruled by Queen Catherine's father, King Ferdinand of Aragon. Somewhat less powerful, but still important, were England and the Holy Roman Empire, which was ruled by the Emperor Maximilian. (It has been remarked by more than one historian that the Holy Roman Empire was not well named, since it was not holy, not Roman, and not an empire. It was a collection of Middle European states, most of them German, loosely held together by the authority of an elected ruler known as the emperor.) Behind England and the Holy Roman Empire came the other, lesser states of Europe.

The principal purpose that had guided King Henry VII in promoting the engagement of Princess Catherine of Aragon to Prince Arthur was to obtain Spain as an ally against the growing power of France. France and England had been bitter rivals ever since 1337, when King Edward III of England had laid unsuccessful claim to the throne of France. From then, until 1453, there had been almost constant fighting between the English and the French—a struggle usually referred to as the Hundred Years' War. Now France was beginning to show signs of renewing the war, and something had to be done.

The current head of the Roman Catholic Church was Pope Julius II, who was as much a warrior as a churchman. Italy, at that time, was not one country at all but a collection of small states which Pope Julius wanted to unite under his own control. He started the process by invading the Duchy of Ferrara, just south of Venice, near the head of the Adriatic Sea. The Duke of Ferrara was a friend and ally of King Louis XII of France, so a French army invaded Italy, while King Louis raised a loud cry for "the reformation of the Church, both in its head and its members." For his part, Pope Julius called upon the Christian princes of Europe to unite in a Holy League to defend the Church and mend the split that King Louis was threatening.

Burning with religious zeal, King Henry VIII came to the assistance of the head of the Church. Wolsey backed his royal master and volunteered to take charge of food and supplies for the fighting men, a valuable activity which would also make possible a private profit for him. Henry also had a private goal in mind. While fighting to protect the Church and the Holy Father, he might very well have a chance to fulfill the ancient dream of Edward III and make good for England her claim to the throne of France.

Other rulers had their own reasons. In Spain, King Ferdinand invited King Henry to send English troops to Spain to join the Spanish soldiery in an invasion of France, for the purpose of conquering Guienne. This was tempting, for the Duchy of Guienne, not far from the Spanish border, was a part of France that Edward III and later English kings had claimed as theirs by feudal right. It was especially for this region that the Hundred Years' War had been undertaken. Actually, King Ferdinand had no interest at all in Guienne. He was planning to conquer and add to his Spanish territories the independent kingdom of Navarre, which lay between Spain and France.

King James IV of Scotland, though he was married to Princess Margaret of England, saw in King Henry's adventure on the mainland a chance to take some English lands along the Scottish-English border. He also wanted to square an account with his regal brother-in-law, who had refused to send to sister Margaret some valuable jewels which her father had left her. As a first step, he unleashed against English seaborne trade a small fleet of privateer warships under three Scottish pirates, the Barton brothers. Soon English ships and cargoes began to disappear at sea.

King Henry's army set sail for Spain in June 1512. The king did not go with them, but traveled to Southampton to see them depart. Though he was not a good sailor, he never failed to thrill at the sight of great warships and galleys, such as those accompanying his transports. He wished them Godspeed, then returned to his castle to await tidings of victory.

There was no victory. King Ferdinand had laid his plans cleverly. The English troops were stationed at the Spanish end of a pass cutting through the mountains between France and Spain. Here, their very presence served to prevent a French invasion of Spain while Ferdinand was taking Navarre. When Navarre had been taken, the Spanish king lost interest in the war and made a separate treaty with Louis XII. When word of this reached the English encampment, the army started home in disgust. They had done nothing for England, nothing for the Pope or the Church. Only Ferdinand had profited by their trip into his country.

Though Ferdinand had signed a treaty with France, Henry had not, nor had he made peace with Scotland. With King Henry as a figurehead, Thomas Wolsey began to reorganize the war effort on a more efficient basis. Under his direction, the army and the navy were quickly brought to a state of readiness.

There had already been action at sea. While the English expeditionary force was still in Spain, word of the raids by the Scottish Barton brothers was brought to King Henry's Council. Sir Thomas Howard, the Earl of Surrey, arose and exclaimed, "The King of England should not be imprisoned in his kingdom while either he has an estate to set up a ship or a son to command it." Then, acting on his own, he fitted out two warships and sent them out under the command of two of his sons. Patrolling in the English Channel, the two Howards encountered and engaged two privateers under the command of Andrew Barton. Thomas Howard, the earl's oldest son, attacked Barton's flagship, the *Lion*, and succeeded in capturing it after a hard-fought battle at close range. As the English sailors came swarming aboard, they found Andrew Barton, mortally wounded, dying on the bloody deck. The other Howard vessel had taken the other privateer. This largely removed the menace of the Scottish seaborne activities.

The French navy, though, was not so easily disposed of. In mid-August 1512, Sir Edward Howard led a squadron of fifty-one English ships in a surprise raid on the French seaport of Brest. The time of the raid was well chosen, for civilians from the town were visiting the French squadron of twenty-one vessels which lay in the harbor. There was no time to ferry the guests ashore. The French admiral, the Sieur de Clermont, ordered the anchors up and the sails set. Still encumbered with hundreds of frightened men and women from the town, the French vessels moved into the outer bay in an effort to save Brest from bombardment. When it became evident that the English would not attack before dark, he anchored his ships, leaving his now-unwelcome guests to make the best they could of a very uncomfortable situation. Howard, too, anchored his squadron to await the dawn before going into action.

When the sun came up, Admiral Clermont was able to see, for the first time, how many English ships he was facing. Fifty-one against twenty-one! The odds were too great. As the English vessels started to move toward him, he ordered his squadron back into the harbor, leaving his largest ship, the *Cordelière*, to cover his retirement.

Captain Portznoguer of the *Cordelière* had his gunners concentrate their sixteen big cannons on the English flagship, *Mary Rose*. She was smashed so badly that she was driven onto the rocks. The real opponent, though, was the *Regent*, the largest of the English ships and fourth in line. Adroitly skirting the already-ruined *Mary Rose* and the two ships which had been close behind her, the French admiral drove his vessel along the *Regent*'s side. French sailors bound the two great ships together. A bloody battle ensued, each ship blasting at the other at a range of mere feet, or even inches. Early in the action, Thomas Knyvet, the *Regent*'s captain, was torn in two by a cannonball, but his death did not halt the mutual slaughter of brave seamen. Both ships took fire and both blew up. Witnesses reported that as his ship exploded beneath him, Captain Portznoguer jumped overboard in full armor and vanished beneath the waves.

The captain and his men had not died in vain. Dismayed by the loss of their flagship and their largest warship, the English gave up the attack and withdrew. Brest and the twenty warships in its harbor had been saved.

Sir Edward Howard promptly dispatched a sealed secret message to Thomas Wolsey, informing him of the doleful results of the raid. Wolsey informed King Henry, then wrote to Bishop Fox. His letter to the bishop ended with the words, "Keep this tidings secret to yourself, for there is no living man knoweth the same here but only the King and I."

It would not do to let the English people know of their loss until there was some encouraging news to counteract it. At once, work was started on a great new warship to replace the two that had been lost. She would be a new flagship for the fleet and a much larger and mightier warship than England had ever had before. She carried twice as many guns as the *Regent,* and her tonnage was half again as great. At bow and stern, the forecastle and aftercastle towered up to dizzy heights, making her, technically, a "high-charged galleon." Her dozen or more great sails of golden cloth were supported by four towering masts. She is said to have carried 184 guns, though only 21 of these were of the largest size, capable of throwing the heaviest projectiles. The others were light "man-killers," each operated by a single gunner. This monstrous ship was appropriately named for her king, *Henri Grâce à Dieu,* though most of King Henry's subjects insisted on calling her the *"Great Harry."*

Brest remained in French hands for the remainder of the war—

blockaded, relatively useless, but safe. It was the scene of only one other bit of naval action. A sharp-eyed sailor in the upper-works of one of the British warships detected six French galleys lying at anchor in the exposed outer bay, in the lee of some small rocky islands. His eyes were not quite sharp enough, though, to detect the presence of hidden cannons on the islands. A fast, unexpected raid might well serve to cut out and capture the six, thus weakening the French fleet and strengthening the English.

Sir Edward Howard led the raid, taking with him only two galleys and four longboats. The results were disastrous. Just as Howard and sixteen followers leaped aboard the largest of the French galleys, the hidden batteries on the rocks blazed forth. In the confusion, Howard's own galley veered away, leaving the seventeen boarders on the French vessel. The fight was short and sharp. Howard and his men were forced overboard, in full armor, and plunged at once to the bottom of the harbor.

To this point, King Henry had taken little personal part in the war. Now, suddenly, he decided to get for himself a share of martial glory and honor. A new Pope, Leo X, was organizing a league against France, and King Henry and Emperor Maximilian promptly joined.

The attack on France by the Pope's League could hardly be termed an outstanding success. King Henry and his army sailed from Dover to Calais late in June 1513. Nearly a month later, he moved against the small walled city of Thérouanne, which was a trade competitor of some of the emperor's cities. Some weeks later, the emperor himself appeared with a small force to help in the siege. Thérouanne surrendered after six weeks and was looted and burned. A Swiss army advanced from the south toward Paris, for the purpose of helping King Henry and the emperor take Paris, but, instead of cooperating, the king and the emperor laid seige to Tournai, another trading city. Disgusted, the Swiss made peace with the French and went home. Tournai surrendered within a month. It was now late September, too late in the year to begin a campaign against Paris, so the royal warriors took their forces and went home. The emperor profited a little through the elimination of Thérouanne, and Thomas Wolsey received a new source of income when the Pope appointed him Bishop of Tournai. King Henry, having spent enormous sums, had accomplished remarkably little for himself or for his country.

While King Henry had been pointlessly campaigning on the continent, events of vast importance had been occurring in England. On August 22, King James IV of Scotland, despite the pleas of his wife, who was King Henry's sister Margaret, had crossed the Tweed River and invaded England. Queen Catherine, though six months pregnant, ordered the Earl of Surrey north to the border with his troops and she personally led a second army to reinforce her general. Because she was so near the time of giving birth, she stopped at Woburn and sent her army on to aid Surrey.

At the beginning of the campaign there was little to choose between the two armies. The Scots had nearly sixty thousand men—nearly twice the English force—but the English were better trained and better disciplined. As the preliminary maneuvering went on, though, the Scots' numerical advantage began to disappear. There were numerous desertions, most of them caused by "the great cold, wind, and wet."

The armies came together at Flodden Field. The Scots had been camping on Flodden Hill, nearby, but on the day of battle —September 9, 1513—they burned their huts and came down from their hillside encampment onto the chosen field. Because of their silent advance and the thick smoke from the fires on the hillside, the two armies were within a quarter of a mile of each other before either discovered the other's presence.

Battle of Flodden Field, September 9, 1513. (Painting by John F. Campbell)

Seeing the orderly English ranks, several of the Scottish nobles urged their king to withdraw and fight at another time under better conditions. One who was especially vehement was Lord Lindsay, who long before had given King James's father, James III, the gray war-horse that had fallen on him in the battle of Canglor. James IV was enraged at hearing such advice from such a man. He ordered his gunners to open the battle.

The Scottish artillery proved to be no match for the English in speed or accuracy. Soon the master gunner of the Scots was dead, and his men had been driven from their guns. As the battle turned against them, the Scots became increasingly frantic. In the end, there was a great charge upon the English center. Some of the Scots were so enraged that they cast aside their shields and swords and fought with their bare hands.

The results were disastrous. Scotsmen fell by the score. King James IV, fighting in the forefront, tried to make his way through to the Earl of Surrey. When scarcely a spear's length away, he went down, his head split by a battle-axe, his side pierced by an arrow, his striking arm half severed by a sword slash. His men grouped about his body and defended it until darkness ended the fighting. Only then did they leave the field, retreating slowly northward.

The news soon reached Queen Catherine by mounted courier, and she at once sat down to write a full report to her beloved husband, King Henry. Her pride in the army that had fought at Flodden Field and in her own very considerable part in smashing back the Scottish invasion was evident throughout her letter:

*Woburn*
*September 16, 1513*

Sir:
*My Lord Howard hath sent me a letter open to Your Grace within one of mine, by the which you shall see the great victory that our Lord hath sent your subjects in your absence, and for this cause, it is no need herein to trouble Your Grace with long*

*writing; but to my thinking, this battle hath been to Your Grace, and all your realm, the greatest honor that could be, and more than should you win all the crown of France. Thanked be God of it, and I am sure Your Grace forgetteth not to do this; which shall be cause to send you many more victories as, I trust, He shall do.*

*My husband—for hastiness with Rouge-cross, I could not send Your Grace the piece of the King of Scots' coat, which John Glyn now bringeth. In this, Your Grace shall see how I can keep my promise, sending you for your banners a king's coat. I thought to send himself to you, but our Englishmen would not suffer it. It should have been better for him to have been in peace, than to have this reward. All that God sendeth is for the best. My Lord of Surrey, my Henry, would fain know your pleasure in burying the King of Scots' body; for he hath written to me so. With the next messenger, Your Grace's pleasure may be herein known; and with this I make an end, praying God to send you home shortly; for without this, no joy here can be accomplished, and for the same I pray. And now I go to our Lady at Walsingham, that I promised so long ago to see.*

*I send Your Grace herein a bill found in a Scottish man's purse, of such things as the French King sent to the said King of Scots to make war against you. Beseeching you to send Matthew hither, as soon as this messenger cometh to bring me tidings from Your Grace.*

*Your humble wife and true servant,*
*Catherine*

Undoubtedly, King Henry felt some irritation at the tone of the letter, emphasizing, as it did, the greater importance of the victory over the Scottish invaders than of his own campaign against the French. Nevertheless, the news was so good, and the accomplishment so genuine, that he could afford to be magnanimous. Thomas Howard, Earl of Surrey, was rewarded by having his former title, Duke of Norfolk, restored to him. Henry's companion Charles Brandon was raised from the rank of commoner and made Duke of Suffolk. Even his brother-in-law, King James IV, who had been excommunicated—cut off from the church—

by the Pope for breaking a treaty by his invasion of England, received consideration. Said King Henry, soberly, "He has paid a heavier penalty for his perfidy than we would have wished." Being excommunicated, King James could not be buried in holy ground without the Pope's permission, so Henry sent a letter to Rome requesting the permission of Leo X to bury the Scottish king in St. Paul's. The request was granted, but before word of this was received the Scots had given up the idea. The body of the unfortunate king lay for years in a storeroom in the palace and eventually disappeared, no one knows where.

The enthusiasm over the victories won against France and Scotland was by no means shared by the intellectual leaders of England. These men had placed great hope in King Henry VIII, but now they saw that he had led his country back into the Hundred Years' War. Dean John Colet of St. Paul's took his life in his hands when he declared in a bitter sermon, "An unjust peace is better than the justest war. . . . When men, out of hatred and ambition, fight with and destroy one another, they fight under the banner, not of Christ but of the Devil."

Erasmus went even further. Though it cost him his professorship at Cambridge University, he boldly declaimed: "It is the people who build cities, while the madness of princes destroys them. . . . Of all birds, the eagle alone has seemed to wise men the type of royalty, a bird neither beautiful nor musical nor good for food, but murderous, greedy, hateful to all, the curse of all, and with its great powers of doing harm only surpassed by its desire to do it."

Sir Thomas More, who had helped to instruct King Henry in his earlier years, was especially disappointed in the backward turn which England was taking. In his book *Utopia,* he described a country where all is as it should be, where there is justice for all, where goodness and virtue lead to success, where everyone works and everyone shares, where crime is prevented rather than punished, where intelligence takes the place of violence. In his gentle way, More was chiding not only England but all of the leading nations of his day, for the name *Utopia* comes from two Greek words meaning "nowhere."

Peace came soon after the victories against the Scots and the French, but the responsibility for it can be credited far more to King Louis XII of France than to the sermons and writings of the idealists. Louis was hard pressed by the coalition against him, so he set about destroying it. He had two valuable assets to bargain with—a daughter named Renée and a claim to the Duchy of Milan, in Italy. Two of his enemies were related to Prince Charles of Spain, who was a grandson of both the Emperor Maximilian of the Holy Roman Empire and of Spain's King Ferdinand. King Louis offered Renée in marriage to Prince Charles with the understanding that Charles was to receive the claim to the Duchy of Milan as part of the marriage bargain. Both of the royal grandfathers were pleased by this and made peace. Seeing this, Pope Leo X also hastened to make peace with France.

Word of the collapse of his coalition first reached King Henry VIII through the Duke of Longueville, one of the distinguished French leaders who had been captured in battle and had been brought back to England as both a guest and a prisoner. During the months of his involuntary visit, the duke had become a favored friend of King Henry. In their conversations, he built up in Henry's mind a desire to make peace with France. He also said that King Louis wished to make peace with England. Since the French queen, Anne of Brittany, had recently died, leaving King Louis without a direct male heir, he wanted a new wife, by whom he might have a son. If King Henry would provide a bride of royal ancestry and with a sufficient dowry, King Louis would gladly make peace with England and would also pay, over a ten-year period, the million crowns which France had owed

England since the signing of a treaty in 1491 but had never intended to pay.

King Henry agreed and offered his young sister, Princess Mary, as Louis's bride. Mary was sixteen, and King Louis was fifty-three. Moreover, she was in love with her brother's friend Charles Brandon, the recently ennobled Duke of Suffolk. Whatever Mary felt had to be sacrificed for the good of her country and the furtherance of King Henry's aims.

The terms were agreed upon, and peace was made. Princess Mary was given a dowry of 400,000 crowns, which would go to her new husband, and they were married at Greenwich Palace on the seventh of August 1514. King Louis was not present; the Duke of Longueville served as proxy for the groom. Somehow, the new Queen of France delayed her journey to her adopted country for two months, but in October she crossed the channel accompanied by the Duke of Norfolk (Thomas Howard), the Duke of Suffolk (her sweetheart, Charles Brandon), and many attendants, including Anne Boleyn, the maid of honor. Upon their arrival in France, a second marriage was held, this time with King Louis present and a French cardinal presiding.

On January 1, 1515—less than three months after his wedding —Louis XII died. Charles Brandon was still at hand, serving as an ambassador to the French court. Within about two months, Queen Mary and Brandon were secretly married. When King Henry learned of the marriage, he expressed strong disapproval, but soon all was forgiven.

# 5
# THE EMPIRE SEEKERS

THE conduct of the war against France and the creation of the "great and lasting peace," which was supposed to have been guaranteed by the marriage of Princess Mary to King Louis XII, were largely achievements of Thomas Wolsey. Not only was Wolsey a successful statesman; he was also a rising churchman. His latest bishopric, Tournai, was his third, and there was every prospect of gaining more, each yielding valuable income. Still, Wolsey was dissatisfied, for William Warham, Archbishop of Canterbury, still outranked him as the highest churchman in the land.

In September 1515, Pope Leo X appointed Thomas Wolsey to the College of Cardinals. Two months later, the red hat of his new office reached Dover and was borne in triumph to London by a host of his followers "as though the greatest prince of Christendom had come into the realm." As the only English cardinal, Wolsey now outranked Warham.

The "great and lasting peace" showed signs of coming to an end within five years. In January 1519, Emperor Maximilian died, leaving the Holy Roman Empire without a ruler. It was up to the seven German noblemen who held the title of elector to choose someone of royal blood to be King of Germany; the Pope would then bestow the title of emperor upon him. King Henry VIII of England, King Francis I of France, and King Charles I, who had just succeeded his grandfather Ferdinand on the throne of Spain, all hoped to be selected for this important office.

King Charles seemed to have the best chance for election. Some years before, his grandfather, King Ferdinand, had secured from a number of electors the promise of support. Ferdinand was dead, but the electors seemed determined to stand by their pledges. As this became evident, Henry and Francis tended to lean on each other for support. Meetings were planned. King Francis was anxious to join Henry in opposition to Charles, but for some reason Henry held back. At last, they made an agreement that neither would shave his face until their formal meeting had been held. Francis lived up to his side of the bargain, with the result that the wearing of full beards became stylish and almost necessary in the French court. Henry went back on his word, and shaved, "because Queen Catherine dislikes bearded chins."

Plots and meetings to the contrary, King Charles I of Spain became Holy Roman Emperor Charles V on June 28, 1519, through the action of the faithful electors.

Even though Charles had been elected, Cardinal Wolsey proceeded with his plans for a meeting between King Henry and King Francis. The title of emperor was no longer a consideration, but peaceful, cooperative relations between England and France were still of vast importance.

The site chosen for the meeting was at the border between France and what was then the English-owned area of Calais, halfway between the French castle of Ardres and the English castle of Guines. On March 19, 1520—only a week after the meeting had been decided on—a horde of English workmen appeared at the chosen spot and set to work. A record of that time reports that they were there for "the making of a palace before the castle gate of Guines; wherefore there was sent the King's master-mason, master-carpenter, with three hundred masons, five hundred carpenters, one hundred joiners, many painters, glaziers, tailors, smiths, and other artificers, both out of England and Flanders, to the number of two thousand and more."

The workers labored, and the open space selected was transformed into an amazing playground and meeting place for royalty. A temporary palace was erected, with walls of stone and timber, windows of glass, and a roof of canvas. Before it stood an elaborate fountain which, during the meeting, would gush forth three kinds of wine for the guests. There was a palace of art so beautifully proportioned that it looked, to some Italian visitors, as though it had been designed by the great Leonardo da Vinci. The meeting hall itself was a gigantic tent of cloth of gold—a beautiful fabric embroidered with golden thread, from which the entire location and meeting took the name of the Field of the Cloth of Gold. There was a French pavilion to rival the English one. Off to one side were the great dining tents, the archery butts, and a jousting field for tournaments. When the meeting had begun, these principal structures would be surrounded by a veritable sea of lesser but beautiful tents for the housing of nobles, churchmen, and lesser members of the group.

Though the great meeting was planned for the sole purpose of creating lasting peace and brotherly love between King Henry VIII of England and King Francis I of France, there was another person who had to be taken into account. The new Emperor Charles V, who was also King Charles I of Spain, was determined to be included. He feared that King Henry and King Francis would become allies against Spain.

During the building of the meeting place, word was received that Emperor Charles was planning a trip from Spain to his possessions in the Netherlands and would like to stop in England to confer with King Henry. An invitation was duly extended, provided the visit would come before King Henry and his retinue should set sail for Calais.

Charles almost failed to appear. From mid-April to mid-May

1520, he waited and fretted in the Spanish port of Corunna, while an ill wind blew persistently from the wrong direction, preventing him from sailing off toward England. The same wind also kept any word of the emperor's situation from reaching King Henry, who worried and delayed and finally started toward Dover with his retinue, in preparation for sailing to Calais. Fortunately, Cardinal Wolsey had gone ahead to Dover and was there when an impressive Spanish ship appeared in the harbor. Knowing well who must be aboard, the cardinal dispatched hasty word to King Henry, then went out in a small boat to make Emperor Charles welcome and conduct him to comfortable quarters in Dover Castle.

Wolsey's message reached King Henry at Canterbury. With a few attendants, he quickly took off and rode hard toward Dover, arriving late in the evening, when the emperor had already gone to bed. Henry had never met Charles, but this did not keep him from barging into the emperor's room, embracing him warmly, then sitting and talking with him through most of the night. They got along famously. Charles was a small, homely, friendly young man with simple tastes and an excellent mind. He was very evidently surprised and pleased by his warm reception, and he showed it. King Henry was no less delighted. This quiet, self-effacing fellow might be an emperor, but unlike tall, athletic, long-nosed Francis I across the Channel he showed no signs of jealous rivalry at all. Agreements and understandings were quickly reached.

The next day, king and emperor rode together back toward Canterbury, where the English royal party was staying in Archbishop Warham's beautiful palace. Here, for the first time in his life, the young emperor met his aunt Queen Catherine, and here, for two more fruitful days, he talked, reasoned, and agreed with King Henry and his great minister, Cardinal Wolsey. Then, on May 29, the entire group departed to the southeast, king and emperor riding together for five miles until they parted at a fork in the road. Emperor Charles proceeded eastward to the port of Sandwich, and King Henry and his company toward Dover.

On the seventh day of June 1520, the French and English kings met on the Field of the Cloth of Gold. There was, at first, a good deal of suspicion, especially on the part of the English. Fears had been voiced that there might be an attack on King Henry VIII, or perhaps an attempt to abduct him. Thus the two kings approached each other warily, each surrounded by his supporters and guards. At the selected spot, a lance had been thrust into the ground. They met beside it, embraced while still on horseback, then dismounted, embraced again, and signaled their followers to come forward and join them within the pavilion.

The first ten days of the meeting were devoted to sports, especially jousting, archery, and the wielding of broadswords. On each such day, both King Henry and King Francis rode against five opponents on the jousting field. In the case of the two kings, there was very little danger. None of their opponents was foolish enough to try to beat a king. Each saw to it that he was knocked from his horse as convincingly as possible, without endangering his regal opponent. The two kings did not ride against one another.

A situation which arose showed well how important it was not to match king against king. Though they were not scheduled to meet in anything except conference and the forging of agreements, the two did meet, at King Henry's suggestion, in an informal contest of archery. Henry, who was good with the bow, managed to win. Inspired by this, he looked for another field in which to show his superiority. He had done a good deal of wrestling, and since he was both larger and stronger than King Francis, he was certain he could beat the French king at that, too. Surprise would help. In a social gathering in his pavilion, in

The meeting between King Francis I of France (*left*) and King Henry VIII of England (*right*) on the Field of the Cloth of Gold, June 7, 1520. (Engraved from a painting by DeBay)

the presence of the two queens and of numerous lords and ladies, he suddenly seized King Francis by the neck, cried, "Brother, let us wrestle!" and attempted to throw him to the ground. Francis, though caught at a disadvantage, was quick and wiry. With a sudden twist, he swung his long, lean leg behind Henry's thick and solid one, heaved mightily, and dumped the English monarch hard upon his neck and shoulders on the floor. Henry came up red, angry, and hot for combat, but the queens saved the day. As one, Queen Catherine and Queen Claude—who had liked each other from their first moment of meeting—stepped forward, gabbling of something, anything! to take the minds of all from what they had just witnessed. Strangely, it worked. There was no more talk of wrestling or of royal combats of any sort.

It is customary to say that nothing at all came from the Field of the Cloth of Gold save huge expenditures and useless playing and feasting. This is almost but not quite true. Although the formal discussions amounted to almost nothing, the meeting was not quite as useless as it seemed, for Cardinal Wolsey had brought together on the Field of the Cloth of Gold the very flower of the French and English nations, to meet in peace and friendship rather than in war. This was something new—something that would set a pattern for other peaceful meetings in the future.

There was another result, too, indirect but important. King Henry and Queen Catherine had come from England aboard the great new warship *Henri Grâce à Dieu*. It had been a frightful voyage. The *"Great Harry"* had pitched and rolled and threatened to go completely over, though the seas had been only moderately rough. The *Henri Grâce à Dieu* was sent to an English navy yard to have something done about her balance. The reason for the trouble was quickly evident. Like other "high-charged galleons," she had many of her heaviest guns mounted in the lofty towers built fore and aft, where they raised the ship's center of gravity much too high for safety. These guns were removed and, with others, were placed on a lower deck behind closable gunports. Now the ship was more heavily armed and steadier. The broadside warship had made its appearance.

King Henry and Queen Catherine did not return to England immediately after the meeting at the Field of the Cloth of Gold. They went instead to Calais, then to Gravelines, just inside the borders of Flanders, which was a part of the Holy Roman Empire. Waiting for King Henry in Gravelines was Emperor Charles V, accompanied by one of his aunts, the Archduchess Margaret of Savoy, Governor of the Netherlands. Together, the emperor and the archduchess accompanied King Henry back to Calais, where they conferred for three days. As before, Charles's quiet, yielding, unassertive manner had a far more favorable influence on Henry than had Francis' all-too-successful attempts to outshine him. The earlier agreements were underscored, and the quiet alliance grew in strength.

Was peace about to descend upon Europe? Edward Hall, one of King Henry's court historians, wrote that while King Henry and King Francis were conferring on June eighteenth on the Field of the Cloth of Gold, "there blew such storms of wind and weather that marvel was to hear; for which hideous tempest some said it was a very prognostication of trouble and hatred to come between princes." Be that as it may, it did blow down a good many tents, rip the roofs from a number of buildings, and terrify many people, and the predicted trouble and hatred were not very long in appearing.

Few men ranked higher among the English nobles than Edward Stafford, the Duke of Buckingham. He was a man of wealth and of ancient family. At the Field of the Cloth of Gold, he was one of the four Honorable Judges of the Jousts. He and his duchess had been received at various of the royal palaces, and they had entertained King Henry and Queen Catherine at Penshurst, their own great country home. The duke's position must have seemed secure.

There were, however, elements of danger in his situation. The Duke of Buckingham was a direct descendant of King Edward III of England and thus had royal blood. His father, when Richard III was king, had stated that he, himself, being of royal lineage, was fit to occupy the throne. For this, he had been seized and executed at King Richard's orders. Now the new duke made the mistake of hiring into his own service one of the king's attendants, Sir William Bulmer. This angered King Henry. The duke also angered Cardinal Wolsey by criticizing his heavy expenditures in staging the pageantry of the Field of the Cloth of Gold.

One must admit that the cardinal was clever in his campaign against Buckingham. He had some of the duke's servants quietly arrested and questioned. None of them said anything damaging. Then he put them on the rack, and when the agony became unbearable they said everything he wanted them to. The cardinal must have known that testimony extracted under torture is undependable, but this did not prevent him from having it all taken down for later presentation to the king. The duke was summoned to London to appear before the king. Suspecting nothing, he went willingly in his ornate barge. On the way, the barge was boarded by officials sent by Wolsey, and the Duke of Buckingham was arrested and taken to the Tower. He remained there for approximately one month. This was no time to trouble King Henry with distressing affairs. May Day was at hand, and the king had made plans with his latest mistress, Mary Boleyn, whose mother, Elizabeth, had also briefly graced the royal bed.

When the holiday was over, the cardinal told the king about the arrest. All of the torture-induced evidence was quoted at length, making Edward Stafford, Duke of Buckingham, sound like the most vicious of traitors.

The trial was held on May 13, 1521. The group of nobles who heard the evidence must have doubted a good deal of it, but with the king and the cardinal pressing for a guilty verdict it would not be safe to say so. The duke was convicted and sentenced to be beheaded. Knowing the pressure that his fellow nobles in the court had been under, he forgave them, saying, "May the eternal God forgive you my death, as I do. I shall never sue to the King for life, howbeit he is a gracious prince, and more grace may come from him than I deserve."

The grace was not forthcoming. The Duke of Buckingham was beheaded four days later. His lands and his wealth went to King Henry VIII, whose vast inheritance from his father was almost gone.

At about this time, events were taking place in Germany

that were to have a great effect on Henry VIII and his place in history. Martin Luther was a monk and was also a professor of theology at the University of Wittenberg. In 1517, a representative of the Catholic Church came to Wittenberg to raise money for a great new cathedral which Pope Leo X was having built in Rome. In his zeal, the representative made promises that the Pope might well not have approved. He promised that anyone who contributed a large sum for the building would be granted an "indulgence," which was an official forgiveness of sin that would excuse the contributor, or some relative or friend already dead, from part of his scheduled punishment in the afterlife. This was more than Luther could stand. He violently condemned this "selling of indulgences," as he called it, and he drew up a series of statements criticizing ninety-five beliefs and practices of the Church with which he disagreed. A copy of these "Ninety-Five Theses" was tacked to the door of the Castle Church of Wittenberg, accompanied by a written offer to debate any of them in public with anyone. This was a usual method of spreading news and information in those days. Another copy was sent directly to Luther's superior in the Church, Archbishop Albrecht of Mainz. Other copies, in German, were soon circulated among the people.

At first, Pope Leo X tried to disregard Luther's objections, but as word spread through Europe this proved to be impossible. To find what Luther really believed, the Pope sent a learned churchman to debate with him. The debate was held, and the churchman was horrified to discover that Luther's beliefs were much like those of John Huss, a religious rebel who had been burned at the stake for heresy in 1415. The Pope ordered Luther to renounce the things he had said and written. Luther not only refused to do so, but he also burned the Pope's order, for which he was promptly excommunicated—cut off from the Church—by Leo X.

King Henry was shocked and angered to see the Holy Father

and the Church so openly defied, and he expressed his willingness to help against such attacks. Cardinal Wolsey was quick to accept. It might help to gain for King Henry a title to match those of the King of France ("Most Christian King") and the Emperor Charles V ("Holy Roman Emperor" and "Most Catholic King"). It might even help Cardinal Wolsey achieve his ambition of becoming the next pope! Henry had written some religious essays in the past. Why not expand these in a book supporting the Pope and opposing Martin Luther?

King Henry promptly set a number of people to work. Sir Thomas More, Bishop John Fisher, Archbishop Edward Lee, Bishop John Longland, and others were soon busy searching for pertinent quotations, translating passages from the Hebrew, and doing other helpful tasks. Though the others did most of the work, King Henry had the first word and the last. His earlier writings, expanded and smoothed, became the first two chapters, retitled "Of Indulgences" and "Of the Pope's Authority." The overall title of the book was *The Defence of the Seven Sacraments.*

In July 1521, the book was finished and printed. Thirty copies were sent to Rome. The Pope was grateful for any help he could get, and he appreciated the fact that the book was dedicated to him. With papal approval, it was translated into a number of European languages. King Henry was rewarded by a new title for himself, "Defender of the Faith." Though the Pope had intended to bestow this title only upon King Henry, and not upon his descendants and successors, the king ignored the restriction. Twenty-two years later, Parliament officially bestowed the title on the rulers of England.

In the summer of 1521, King Henry's attention shifted from questions of religion to matters of international intrigue. Emperor Charles was finding it difficult to do full justice to the two titles which he held—Emperor Charles V of the Holy Roman Empire

Holy Roman Emperor Charles V (*second from left*) and King Francis I of France (*second from right*). (Painting by Baron Antoine Jean Gros)

and King Charles I of Spain. The people of Spain were unhappy, feeling that their country was being neglected in favor of the loose federation of German states which made up the other part of Charles's holdings. Bitter criticism was heard, and an armed uprising of Spaniards against their king seemed possible.

King Francis I seized happily upon the presumed troubles in Spain. A French army launched a sudden attack across the Pyrenees and, in a little more than two weeks, conquered Navarre, which Spain had taken from France only nine years earlier.

The Spaniards quickly forgot their quarrel with Charles and rallied to repel the Frenchmen. Navarre was reconquered almost as quickly as it had been lost. The war settled into a balance, with neither side having a firm advantage. Messages reached King Henry from both Charles and Francis, asking his aid as an ally.

Because of a shortage of money and the lateness of the season, King Henry was not ready to launch an immediate attack upon either of the combatants. Instead, he set up a peace conference at Calais and sent Cardinal Wolsey to represent him. The cardinal took with him Sir Thomas More and Cuthbert Tunstall, Bishop of London. King Henry and Wolsey had already decided in favor of Emperor Charles, who was also receiving support from the Pope, but they wanted to preserve an appearance of fairness and to use up as much time as possible before English intervention.

In the midst of the meeting, Cardinal Wolsey inconspicuously slipped away and traveled to Bruges to confer with Emperor Charles and lay plans for eventual English help. The conference lasted nearly two weeks and covered a wide variety of subjects, ranging from detailed plans for military cooperation to the engagement of Emperor Charles, who was now twenty-two years old, to marry King Henry's daughter, six-year-old Princess Mary. The fact that Mary was already betrothed to the Dauphin of

France merely added one more bit of hidden intrigue to the affair.

Cardinal Wolsey returned to Calais to rejoin the conference. He then hurried back to King Henry with the information that the emperor and the Pope were in the right and should be aided. As soon as it could be managed, England would send an army of 40,000 men to make war on the French.

In November 1521—even before England was actively in the war, the armies of Pope and emperor retook Milan and Tournai from the French. Pope Leo X, overjoyed at the freeing of the great Italian city of Milan, organized a triumphal celebration. In the midst of it, he died. A new Pope had to be chosen. Cardinal Wolsey wanted to be Pope and King Henry supported him, but Emperor Charles favored a little-known Belgian, who was elected and took office as Pope Adrian VI.

King Henry had never given up the idea that, as King of England, he had a valid claim to the French crown as well. In the summer of 1522, war was officially declared against France, and an army was sent to Calais to launch an invasion. Money was scarce, for the inheritance from Henry VII had been spent. Wolsey had the task of raising the needed funds but the war was unpopular. War with France meant war with Scotland, and few Englishmen wanted another series of raids across the border. Demands for gifts, or "benevolences," from the citizens yielded little, and at last the cardinal had to summon Parliament. The members were unwilling to vote money for the war. Sir Thomas More, serving as Speaker, was called upon to answer for Parliament. He bowed low and said that he had no power to say anything without the approval of the members. In the end, Wolsey had to settle for less than half of what he had demanded.

As expected, the Scots went to war to help the French. As their raids began, Thomas Howard, the Earl of Surrey, struck back at them with a little army of only nine thousand men. The Duke of Albany, leader of the Scots, had more men, but his morale was ruined by the thought that it was Surrey who had brought such ruin upon another Scottish army on Flodden Field. Despite the odds, Surrey advanced, his army being swelled by reinforcements as he went. The Duke of Albany fell back before him, refusing to give battle. Surrey then laid waste the country-side north of the border so that it could support no more Scottish raiders. A report to Cardinal Wolsey states, "The Earl of Surrey hath so devastated and destroyed all Tweedale and March, that there is left neither house, fortress, village, tree, cattle, corn, or other succour for man; insomuch that some of the people that fled . . . were compelled to come into England begging bread. . . . And with no imprisonment, cutting off their ears, burning them in their faces, or otherwise can be kept away."

The disgraceful retreat of the Duke of Albany lost him his command and caused him to flee to France. In the confusion that followed, Scottish Queen Margaret, sister of Henry VIII, was able to seize power and restore her son, James V, to the throne. Peace was made, and the border war came to an end.

King Francis, confident that the Scots would keep the English busy at home, led his forces south into Italy against a league of Italian cities allied with the emperor and the Pope. As he left France relatively undefended, the English army invaded from the Calais area, advancing to within less than fifty miles of Paris. Just when it appeared that the French capital would be taken without too much trouble, the invaders halted their advance and retired to Calais. The invasion was supposed to be a two-pronged attack, but Emperor Charles had failed to lead his armies out of Italy against the French.

There were a number of reasons for the failure of the Empire forces to advance: poor planning, shortage of money, lack of initiative. The principal reason, though, was Church politics.

Poor Pope Adrian, after two years of trying to conduct his high office as an honest man should, was dying of exhaustion and frustration. To Emperor Charles, the selection of the right man to replace him was far more important than helping King Henry defeat France.

To be sure, the emperor had promised Wolsey all possible aid in winning the papacy. To keep the English army active in the field against King Francis, he had to appear to do just that, so he drew up orders to his representatives in Rome to make every effort and exert all possible influence to secure the English cardinal's election. Copies of these orders were sent to Wolsey. What Wolsey did not see was one more order to stop the messenger and take from him the papers concerning Wolsey. Emperor Charles wanted a pope who would be easier to control than Wolsey. He had long had such a man in mind, Cardinal Giulio de' Medici, who had been an assistant to Pope Leo X. It took a month of politics and persuasion, but de' Medici was elected. There then remained only one barrier. The successful candidate was illegitimate, but a vote by the College of Cardinals made him officially legitimate, and he assumed his high, holy office under the name of Clement VII.

Cardinal Wolsey knew at once that he had been betrayed. Although his armies had been on the verge of taking Paris, he promptly withdrew them, explaining that the men were suffering from "the extreme cold and other sore weathers," with many losing "their fingers, hands, and feet, being frozen dead upon their beds, and some daily cut off." One master of deceit had met another, and an important military campaign was lost after having been virtually won.

The war itself, though, had not been lost. In the spring of 1524, the emperor's armies, commanded by the Duke of Bourbon, put such pressure on the French invaders of Italy that they withdrew. Then King Francis reinvaded, besieging Pavia in the late summer and early fall. The war hung in the balance until Francis divided his force, leading half his army south to attack Naples. The imperial forces followed him, and a great battle was fought at Pavia on February 24, 1525. The French lost, and King Francis himself was captured.

The capture of the French King revived King Henry's ambition to gain the throne of France in addition to that of England. This would take money. The king and Wolsey distrusted Parliament. Instead, they went to the people, demanding that each man pay one sixth of everything that he owned. The people protested. It was the employees of the Suffolk clothing makers who brought the matter to an end by flatly refusing to pay. Large numbers of them gathered under the lead of a man named John Greene, ready to resist to the death this new and illegal form of robbery by their own government.

The Duke of Suffolk decided that they should be forced to pay on pain of death. The Duke of Norfolk, Admiral of England and Lord High Treasurer, had a better idea. Backed by a strong but restrained body of troops, he appeared before the assembled people and asked who their captain was. John Greene spoke up. "My Lord," he said, "sith you ask who is our captain, forsooth his name is Poverty, for he and his cousin Necessity hath brought us to this doing. The clothmakers have put all these people and a far greater number from work; the husbandmen have put away their servants and given up household; they say the King asketh so much that they be not able to do as they have done before this time, and then, of necessity, must we die wretchedly. Wherefore, my Lord, according to your wisdom, consider our necessity."

The Duke of Norfolk had sufficient wisdom to consider their necessity and did so thoughtfully. Upon his return to London, he presented their case to King Henry and Cardinal Wolsey so well that they could see at once the unfairness and the danger of collecting such a tax. The king pretended not to know that such a demand had been made upon the people, thus shifting the entire blame to Wolsey. The tax of one sixth was canceled and those who had gathered to resist were forgiven. Instead, "benevolences" were laid upon the rich, who complained but paid. The money raised was not sufficient to launch another war against France for possession of King Francis' crown.

The war of King Henry and Emperor Charles against Francis I of France ended in complete confusion. Henry and Charles quarreled bitterly. The English king wanted the emperor to help him get the throne of France. Charles refused. Henry then demanded that the captive French king be turned over to him, to be held as his prisoner. This, too, was refused, though Francis continued to be a prisoner, first in Italy, later in Spain. Then Henry demanded money, but Charles had none to spare. Changing the subject, he protested that his engagement to Princess Mary had been broken without his knowledge or consent and that his ambassador had been insulted in London. The result was the dissolution of the alliance of the English king and the emperor against France.

King Francis was released after a full year of captivity. To gain his freedom, he had had to promise the Duchy of Burgundy to the emperor, but when he had crossed into France, declaring "Now I am a king again!" he refused to give up the territory. In this double-dealing he was encouraged by King Henry VIII, who advised him to give the emperor nothing, and by Pope Clement VII, who used his divine influence to cancel the oath which had been sworn.

Suddenly, Charles V found himself without friends. It had occurred to Henry VIII, Francis I, and Pope Clement VII that the empire was growing too strong and that the safest plan was to oppose it, with the help of as many friends and allies as possible.

One would have thought that Pope Clement would be the last of the three to clash with the Holy Roman Emperor, but he was the first. One must remember that then popes were not only the spiritual leaders of the strongest and most influential Church in Europe, but also feudal lords with lands, castles, and followers. The Pope's quarrel with the emperor came partly from his spiritual leadership and partly from his position as a great landowner in Italy. Though he was distressed by the growing number of "heretic Lutherans" in Germany, he was also distressed by the emperor's claims to extensive Italian territories. Clement bitterly denounced the emperor, and the emperor urged his own followers to strike back at the Pope.

Two empire armies started for Italy, under the overall command of the Duke of Bourbon. The Pope tried to stop them by excommunicating the Duke of Bourbon and invoking God's help against the "heretic Lutheran Germans" and the "Mohammedan Spaniards" who were attacking him. Such tactics had little effect. The armies laid siege to Rome. The Duke of Bourbon was killed as he tried to mount a scaling ladder, but even his death did not halt the attackers. They captured Rome and looted it, while the Pope and a group of his followers took refuge in the castle of Sant'Angelo.

The emperor's government, meanwhile, was conducting a strange double series of activities. Throughout the land, prayer services were being held for the safety of the great spiritual leader, while at the same time the armies were being urged on against the great Italian landowner. To some, this smacked of hypocrisy; to the less critical, it was merely a way of differentiating between the Pope as the spiritual leader and the Pope as a feudal landlord.

When Cardinal Wolsey tried to talk King Henry into going to the aid of the Pope, the king is reported to have said, "I more lament this evil chance than my tongue can tell, but when you say that I am 'Defender of the Faith,' I assure you that this war between the Emperor and the Pope is not for the Faith but for temporal possessions and dominions."

While Italy was being invaded and Rome sacked, King Francis visited King Henry in England to work out the details of a treaty between them and against a Holy Roman Empire that had grown too strong. Many proposals were made and accepted, concerning military cooperation, the hand of Princess Mary to either King Francis or his second son, payments by Francis to Henry, and the like. When at last the series of conferences was over, a farewell celebration was held. King Henry's partner in this was a delightful young lady who had quite taken his eye and his heart. Her name was Anne Boleyn.

# 6
# A QUESTION OF DIVORCE

ONE often hears it said that King Henry VIII grew tired of Queen Catherine, fell in love with Anne Boleyn, and began to think of divorce. Though there is some truth to this statement, it was not that simple.

By far the most important cause of Henry's interest in a divorce was the urgent need of a son to succeed him on the throne of England. Queen Catherine was six years older than King Henry, and by the early 1520's it seemed clear to Henry that she had lost whatever slight ability she had had to bear healthy children. Her eight pregnancies had produced only a single living child, Princess Mary. To be sure, Henry did have a living son, Henry Fitzroy by name, but he was even less healthy than Princess Mary, being "tysique" (pronounced "sick"), a strange term meaning frail and nervous. Henry Fitzroy had a greater disadvantage, for he was illegitimate, being the son of Elizabeth Blount, one of the king's mistresses. Although an illegitimate son was no improvement over a legitimate daughter as an heir to the throne, King Henry was so desperate that he bestowed the title Earl of Richmond on the boy and named him as his heir.

Anne Boleyn was a charming young English girl, a daughter of Sir Thomas Boleyn. She knew precisely what she wanted, and she had an excellent idea what she must do to get it. She enjoyed many advantages, being physically attractive, small, and graceful. At an early age, she had been sent to France to serve

74

as a lady-in-waiting to Queen Claude. While at the French court, she had learned to sing, to dance, and to converse far better than the English ladies-in-waiting who attended Queen Catherine. It is small wonder that soon after her arrival in England she caught the eye, aroused the interest, and stirred the heart of England's king.

Being a royal mistress was no part of Anne Boleyn's plan. Her mother and her sister Mary had both held that position, and it had done remarkably little for either of them. Anne wanted to be Queen of England. With this in mind, she went out of her way to flirt with the king, permitting him to kiss and caress her, but steadfastly refusing him those further privileges with which her mother and sister had been so free.

Queen Catherine was horrified by the rumors of a possible divorce. She deeply loved her husband, and she had done everything in her power to help him and England rise toward greatness. She wanted to remain queen; perhaps most important of all, she wanted to protect her daughter. If the marriage were to be annulled, as seemed possible, Princess Mary would lose her high position as a princess of the royal family and would become an illegitimate female descendant without rights or status.

Divorce, in the early sixteenth century, presented very different problems from divorce today. The Church was strongly against it: "Whom God hath joined, let no man put asunder." One could not, then, hope to be "unmarried." One could, though, hope to have it proved that one had never been married in the first place, which would produce the same result. The statement in Leviticus that a man must not marry his brother's widow might well provide good grounds for canceling King Henry's marriage to Queen Catherine and freeing the king to marry again.

Cardinal Wolsey was confident that the marriage could be

annulled on these grounds. Prince Arthur's boasts to his friends on the morning after his marriage seemed to indicate a consummation, which would bring the Book of Leviticus into play. Perhaps even stronger evidence was the fate of all but one of the babies which Catherine had conceived as Henry's queen. Seven of the eight, including all of the boys, had been born dead or had quickly died, and Mary, the one girl child who had lived, had never enjoyed good health. "They shall remain childless," said Leviticus. Surely, some great power was working to discredit the marriage!

Queen Catherine had sworn, and would again, that she had come to Henry's bed a virgin, never before having been truly married. She and Henry were therefore legitimately man and wife and could not be separated. Even if this were not believed, Leviticus was not the only book in the Bible that had spoken out on the subject. In the Book of Deuteronomy, the great religious leader Moses is quoted as urging one of his followers to marry his brother's widow. Why was Leviticus any greater authority than Deuteronomy?

In the defense of her marriage, Queen Catherine had a very powerful ally. The Holy Roman Emperor, Charles V, was her nephew. Emperor Charles not only had great influence in the Catholic Church because of his high office and his title, but he was also holding Pope Clement VII a near-prisoner in the castle of Sant'Angelo, in Rome. The Pope was, therefore, in no position to oppose anything the emperor wanted.

As Catherine had hoped, Emperor Charles ordered Pope Clement not to grant a divorce decree, and the Pope obeyed. This, however, did little to restore the queen's husband to her. King Henry was no longer living with her in a husband-wife relationship, and he was seeing more and more of Anne Boleyn.

In the year 1527, King Henry's desire for a divorce became an international matter. In July of that year, Cardinal Wolsey undertook a diplomatic journey to France to discuss with King Francis I and his ministers a number of interrelated questions. Among the items discussed was King Francis' engagement to young Princess Mary of England. Francis was interested in securing a more mature second wife, so it was agreed that Mary should become the bride of Francis' son, the eight-year-old Duke of Orleans. At the same time, the cardinal suggested that if King Henry could secure a divorce from Queen Catherine he might marry Princess Renée of France, a possibility that interested King Francis.

The personal matters being disposed of, the cardinal and the king turned to more important business. Emperor Charles V was still holding Pope Clement a prisoner at Sant'Angelo. King Francis wished to send a French army into Italy to rescue the Pope, and Wolsey agreed, in King Henry's name, to send an English army to cooperate in freeing His Holiness. The agreement was made, even though it meant war against the empire.

When the cardinal returned to England, the king approved all of the agreements he had made, with one exception. Henry indignantly refused to consider marrying Princess Renée. Should he get his divorce, he planned to marry Anne Boleyn.

As agreed, King Francis sent his army of liberation, under General Lautrec, across the Alps into Italy to rescue Pope Clement. At the same time, King Henry was slowly readying an English army to cooperate with the French and hastily preparing a diplomatic mission to seek an audience with the Pope upon his release.

In the meantime, Pope Clement had taken steps in his own behalf. While the French army was still some distance away, he managed to borrow working clothes from one of the groundkeepers of the castle of Sant'Angelo. Thus disguised, he managed to slip away and to reach the fortified city of Orvieto.

Though Orvieto offered safety from the emperor, it presented an embarrassment of quite another kind. King Henry's diplomatic mission was there, and it lost no time in laying a series of strong requests before the Pope. There were two papers to be signed. One would bestow on Cardinal Wolsey the right to hear the evidence concerning King Henry's much-desired divorce and to make a binding decision in the matter. The other—to become effective only if the cardinal decided that a divorce was justified —would grant King Henry the right to take as his second wife any unmarried woman he wished, even if she was engaged to someone else. There were good reasons for these two provisions. King Henry had taken Anne Boleyn from young Henry Percy, son of the Earl of Northumberland. Percy and Anne had been formally engaged, and King Henry did not want that to stand in his way.

Pope Clement knew that the King of England was readying an army to send to his aid against the emperor, and he wished to do nothing to endanger this most-needed help from King Henry. However, the signing of the papers could infuriate Emperor Charles V, for it was his aunt whom Henry was trying to divorce. The emperor was near, and his troops already held most of the papal territories. The Pope signed the papers, saying that he was sacrificing the considerations of prudence to those of gratitude, and that he hoped King Henry would be careful in the use of the papers, for his (Clement's) safety, as perhaps his life, depended upon it.

When the English armies arrived, Pope Clement showed his appreciation by sending one of his key men, Cardinal Campeggio, to England to work with Cardinal Wolsey in judging the merits of King Henry's divorce case against Queen Catherine. The distinguished churchman was not very helpful. After long consideration, all he could suggest was that Queen Catherine retire to a nunnery, leaving the way clear for an uncontested divorce. The queen heard the proposition, thought it over, and agreed with one important reservation. She said she would retire to a nunnery only if King Henry would retire to a monastery. King Henry, of course, refused.

Emperor Charles V and his advisors showed great cleverness in their handling of the English intervention against them on the continent. Knowing of King Henry's stubborn pride and of the high regard in which the English people held him, they blamed the war on Cardinal Wolsey, who was said to be angry because Charles had refused to use his influence to gain Wolsey the papacy. They said that the cardinal had tricked England's king and people into a war they did not really want. While spreading this story, the emperor was doing all in his power to make the war unpopular in England. Corn exports from Flanders to England were forbidden, bringing on a shortage of food in the cities. The people of the Low Countries were forbidden to import manufactured goods from England, which caused great hardship, especially among the clothmakers of London. The campaign worked. In June 1528, England made peace with the empire, although hostilities continued with Charles's other country, Spain.

The emperor's campaign against Cardinal Wolsey was ably assisted by Anne Boleyn. King Henry was now living with her, having abandoned Queen Catherine. As months went by, and the Legatine Court headed by the two cardinals showed no signs of drawing closer to a decision, she found many opportunities to whisper in the king's ear her unfriendly thoughts about Wolsey. When at last Pope Clement revoked the powers of the court, she was able to mutter some very convincing "told you so" comments that greatly influenced the king.

Now that Cardinal Wolsey seemed to be on unsteady ground, other enemies appeared and added their comments to the chorus of criticism. The Dukes of Norfolk and Suffolk and Anne's own father, recently elevated by receiving the title of Viscount Rochford, vied in voicing doubts that the cardinal had ever really cared about the king's interests. They suggested that he had expended his best efforts in building up his own fortune, power, and prestige. There was just enough truth in these accusations to make them extremely damaging.

Although no charges had as yet been brought against the cardinal, he soon discovered the dangers of his situation. He was not abused, but even worse than abuse is neglect when one has been an acknowledged leader. He was no longer invited to court. His advice was no longer sought. Wolsey endured it as long as he could, then humbly requested that the king grant him a personal interview. To the surprise of most of the courtiers and of the cardinal himself, the request was granted.

When the cardinal arrived, it was learned that no quarters had been set aside for him, so he had to depend on a nearby friend for a place to sleep. At the reception itself, he knelt humbly before the king, awaiting a sign. He had not long to wait. King Henry strode forward and helped Wolsey to his feet. The two men then held a long and apparently cordial discussion in voices so low that only they knew what was said. After dinner, they continued to talk, this time in the king's apartment. As Wolsey was leaving for his borrowed quarters, the king was heard to invite him back for a further meeting the next morning.

It was a time of worry and tension for the cardinal's enemies. They need not have worried. Once more, Anne Boleyn succeeded in turning King Henry against Cardinal Wolsey. The king's returning regard for his great minister was extinguished, and he promised Anne that he would never speak to Wolsey again. When the cardinal arrived the next morning, King Henry was just setting out for a day on horseback in the fields. The two men never saw each other again.

Wolsey's enemies now got to work. Legal papers were prepared, charging the cardinal with violating an old law that had

Henry VIII dismissing Cardinal Wolsey, 1529. (Painting by an un-known artist)

been passed during the reign of King Richard II, in the late 1300s—a law which forbade Englishmen to carry a legal appeal beyond the English courts to the Pope. The cardinal offered no defense, though it was doubtful that he had violated the law in question. In the hope of obtaining royal pardon, he even surrendered his lands and prized possessions, valued at some half-million crowns. The king accepted them, leaving the cardinal the use of only the poorest of his houses, at Esher, near Winchester. There Wolsey went to live, even though the house was completely unfurnished and he was without money. Even his beloved jester had to go to serve the king, although he resisted leaving his master until forcibly removed by six strong men.

Still, enemies continued to make further charges against the cardinal. King Henry took no active part in the persecution. He had not forgotten the many services the great minister had rendered, nor was he sure that he wanted to play too active a part in convicting a cardinal while the Church might still be of service to him in the obtaining of a divorce and in certain other matters which he had in mind.

In the end, Wolsey's enemies had their way. While on his way to attend a religious ceremony, the cardinal was arrested and charged with treason. His health was poor, and he now collapsed, becoming too ill to be moved to the Tower of London to undergo punishment.

Leicester Abbey was nearby, and the cardinal was taken there to regain his strength. As he was carried through the gate of the abbey, he was greeted by the Abbot of Leicester. Said Cardinal Wolsey, "Father Abbot, I am come to lay my bones among you."

He was as good as his word. The very next day he died, and he was buried at Leicester.

# 7
# THE BREAK WITH ROME

THE great Cardinal Wolsey was dead. There was little question who should replace him as Chancellor. King Henry's former tutor and long-time companion, Sir Thomas More, was chosen. Two dukes, persistent enemies of the late cardinal, were chosen for other important posts —Suffolk for Earl Marshal and Norfolk for President of the Cabinet. These three and three other less prominent men made up the six-man Privy Council, which would carry out many of the duties that Cardinal Wolsey had handled by himself.

The new governing body began to push forward the cause of King Henry's divorce. By the use of thinly veiled threats, the great English universities of Cambridge and Oxford were persuaded to issue opinions favorable to the issuing of a divorce decree. A direct appeal was made to Pope Clement VII, who confided to his closest associates that while he was quite willing for the decree to be granted by one of his legates, such as Cardinal Campeggio, he, personally, did not want the responsibility of issuing it. The faculty members of the University of Paris failed to agree, but King Francis, seeking Henry's friendship and support, issued a statement which said that both he and the University of Paris favored it. Emperor Charles V was against it, since it was his aunt who was to be divorced. He felt that only the Pope should decide.

While the question of divorce was being considered, there

came into prominence a sinister character who was destined to play an important role in the reign of King Henry VIII. He was Thomas Cromwell, a man of humble beginnings but with burning ambition and a sly sense of strategy. He had been a minor businessman, a trader, a soldier, and a moneylender. Cardinal Wolsey had been among the many prominent men to use Cromwell's dubious talents, and it was Wolsey who had gained him a seat in Parliament in 1523. Later, when the cardinal was on trial for his life, Cromwell served as Wolsey's defender. Not wishing to antagonize the king, he tried convincingly but not quite hard enough to gain acquittal.

One of Cromwell's first maneuvers in his quest of power was to gain, through bribery, the job of administrating the wealth of monasteries being closed by the government. He had done similar work under Cardinal Wolsey, so he knew how to take full advantage of the possibilities of his new assignment: an opportunity to make money for himself and a chance to bring himself to the king's attention. The first of these was routine for Thomas Cromwell. It was the second that he now found particularly exciting.

Sir Thomas More recognized at once both the advantages and the dangers in having a man like Cromwell close to the king. At his first opportunity, he gave this new man some excellent advice: "Master Cromwell, you are now entered into the services of a most noble, wise, and liberal prince. If you will follow my poor advice, you shall, in counsel-giving unto His Grace, ever tell him what he ought to do, but never tell him what he is able to do; so shall you show yourself a true, faithful servant and a right worthy councilor. For if the lion knew his own strength, hard were it for any man to rule him."

Thomas Cromwell completely ignored the advice. At the earliest possible moment, he sought an audience with King Henry, determined by his very boldness and cleverness to "make or mar"

Thomas Cromwell, chief minister of King Henry VIII. (Portrait
c. 1532 by Hans Holbein the Younger)

his chance of gaining real power in the government. What he said during their meeting delighted King Henry: that those who favored the divorce were the ones who mattered—the learned men, the university people, King Francis, and others; that only the timid, the stupid, and those whose power would be lessened by the divorce were showing opposition; that Henry, as sovereign head of the English government, should not accept dictation from Rome but should make himself head of the Christian Church in England; that not only power and privilege were involved in the religious decisions but vast sums of money as well —money now being sent to Rome which should remain in England under the king's control. Almost at once Thomas Cromwell found himself a member of the King's Privy Council.

Henry's take-over of the Church in England was a masterpiece of sly trickery. The old law of Richard II, under which Cardinal Wolsey had been prosecuted and found guilty, was said to apply equally to all clergymen. By serving under the cardinal, accepting his authority, and not denouncing him for his violations, they, too, were guilty and subject to the gravest penalties. Leaders of the horrified clergymen met and offered the king 100,000 pounds if he would grant a full pardon to all. King Henry refused. Were they to die? The king allowed them to worry, then said that he would accept their offer provided they signed a paper acknowledging the king as "the Protector and only Supreme Head of the Church and Clergy of England." Fearful though they were, the churchmen could not reject so completely the authority of Rome. The king's title was changed to read "the Chief Protector, the only and supreme Lord, and, as far as the law of Christ will allow, the Supreme Head." Henry was disappointed, but feeling that the limiting clause could be quietly removed in the future, he accepted the compromise.

Now that Henry's authority had been officially recognized by the clergy, he set about making church matters more to his liking.

Throughout Europe, it was customary for newly appointed clergymen to pay the first year's receipts from his area to the Pope, from whom, directly or indirectly, he had received his appointment. This was abruptly changed. Henceforth, all clergymen were forbidden to send such payments, called annates, out of the country. They were to stay in England, where Henry, as head of the English Church, could use them for his own purposes or in bargaining with the Pope. He was not ready to make a complete break with the Church of Rome, provided the Church would do what he wished concerning the divorce and other matters.

Not all of the important statesmen and churchmen of England were in agreement with King Henry's policies. An outstanding example was Sir Thomas More. Early in his career as chancellor he tried to cooperate with the king despite his qualms of conscience and his growing certainty that the new policies were wrong. The strain proved too great. In May 1532, he resigned the chancellery, after having held it for only a little over two years. He wished to retire from public life to study and meditate, and King Henry let him go, replacing him with Sir Thomas Audley, who did not have so strict a conscience and sense of honesty. As he so often did, King Henry allowed Sir Thomas More to leave without criticism or threat but with some quiet thoughts that would bring little good to Sir Thomas More in the time to come.

William Warham, the conservative old Archbishop of Canterbury, was another who could not tolerate King Henry's new policies, especially those concerning the Church. Whatever influence he had was conscientiously though vainly exerted in favor of maintaining reverence for and cooperation with the Church of Rome. It was perhaps fortunate for him that he died a natural death before he could be questioned about and punished for his thoughts, words, and actions.

King Henry had no doubts about a worthy successor to Archbishop Warham. In the court of Emperor Charles V was Thomas Cranmer, an energetic English clergyman who had been serving as Henry's personal ambassador to the Holy Roman Empire. Cranmer was a close friend of the Boleyn family and a firm supporter of King Henry VIII. It was he who had first made the suggestion that the English universities should be induced to give favorable opinions on the rightness of the king's proposed divorce from Queen Catherine. Later, he had composed a powerful written presentation of the rightness of the king's position in seeking the divorce as a necessary protection of the royal line of descent, since Queen Catherine would be unable to provide a living male heir. In 1530, he had accompanied Thomas Boleyn, the Earl of Wiltshire, to Rome, where he had fearlessly and ably presented his arguments to high Church officials. These activities had caused King Henry to exclaim, "This man has the right sow by the ear." Now was the time for Thomas Cranmer to return to England and turn the Archbishopric of Canterbury into a fortress of great strength for Henry's policies.

King Henry's summons was not an unmixed blessing for Thomas Cranmer. While in Germany, he had fallen in love with a German girl and had married her. The Church position for which he was being recalled should not be filled by a married man, for, in spite of the differences with the Pope, the English Church was still a part of the Roman Catholic Church. He came hesitantly, leaving his wife behind and saying nothing of his marriage. King Henry either did not know of the situation or decided to ignore it. Likewise, there was no difficulty with the Pope. Clement VII, a weary and dying man who still hoped to heal the breach with England, readily confirmed the appointment, thus assuring for his successors a great deal of trouble during the years ahead.

In the meantime, King Henry and Anne Boleyn had taken

Thomas Cranmer, Archbishop of Canterbury. (Portrait, 1546, by Gerlach Flicke)

matters into their own hands. Openly traveling together, they went to France as guests of King Francis, who had placed an unofficial sort of approval on their relationship by dancing with Anne. On their return, they were secretly married by Dr. Rowland Lee, one of the castle chaplains. It was necessary that something be done, for Anne was two months pregnant with what they both hoped was a son and heir.

Now was the time for the new Archbishop of Canterbury to perform the first of the important functions for which he had been brought back to England. Assuming an ignorance which certainly could not have been genuine, he purported to have discovered for himself the distressing situation of a totally invalid marriage between King Henry and Queen Catherine. He expressed shock at the dangers which this situation held for the nation and the royal succession, and he generously offered to look into the matter and to make a decision. King Henry gratefully accepted the offer, which is scarcely amazing since both he and Cromwell had helped draft it.

Queen Catherine was not deceived by Archbishop Cranmer's pious-sounding offer. When summoned to meet with him, she did not appear. Though condemned as being stubbornly disobedient, she also disregarded a second summons, and the archbishop's court proceeded to hear evidence in her absence. After an interval long enough to make it seem that evidence had been carefully weighed, Archbishop Cranmer announced that King Henry's marriage to Queen Catherine was and had always been void and illegal, in direct violation of the divine commandment in Leviticus; that the king should immediately break off all contact with the widow of his brother Arthur; and that Princess Mary, having been born of an illicit union, was in fact illegitimate. This decision left the king free to marry again. Since he had married before the decision, Henry and Anne Boleyn were married again.

Many times since the beginning of the campaign for the divorce, Queen Catherine had said: "I love and have loved my lord, the King, as much as any woman can love a man, but I would not have borne his company as his wife for one moment against the voice of my conscience. I came to him as a virgin, I am his true wife, and whatever proofs others may allege to the contrary, I, who know better than anyone else, tell you are lies and forgeries." From this she never varied and never would to the day of her death. She was, however, helpless against the forces arrayed against her. Even the action of Pope Clement VII and a consistory of cardinals in declaring Cranmer's decisions erroneous and Catherine's marriage to Henry still sound did little for her. It merely hastened the complete break between the Churches of Rome and England. Catherine was officially stripped of her title of Queen on July 5, 1533. Since Anne had already been crowned Queen on June 1, England had had two queens for more than a month.

For two years and a half after ceasing to be queen, Catherine of Aragon lived in unhappy exile in the unpretentious manor of Ampthill. She never ceased expressing her love for her husband, and shortly before she died of dropsy she still maintained that the privilege she desired "above all things" was to see him once again. It was a wish which remained unfulfilled.

As time before the arrival of Queen Anne's baby grew shorter, King Henry became more and more excited. The most elaborate preparations were made to receive the little prince. Only the birth of a legitimate son could rescue the royal succession from the inadequate people now in line of succession—illegitimate Henry Fitzroy and Princess Mary, daughter of repudiated Catherine of Aragon. Anne was the Great Royal Queen. With God's help, she would do her duty and produce a son. Any other outcome was unthinkable.

On September 7, 1533, the unthinkable occurred. Queen

Anne gave birth to a girl baby, who received the name Elizabeth. Henry's fantastic dreamworld, on which he had so unrealistically counted, collapsed about him.

On March 3, 1534, a subservient Parliament passed the Act of Succession, proclaiming Henry's marriage to Catherine invalid and Princess Mary a bastard, naming Princess Elizabeth the heir to the throne unless Queen Anne should produce a royal son, making it a crime punishable by death to question the legality of Henry's marriage to Anne, and requiring an oath of complete loyalty to King Henry.

Regardless of personal feelings, almost everyone accepted the Act of Succession in full, since it could not be avoided and was extremely dangerous to oppose or to resist. There were two notable exceptions: King Henry's long-time friend and former tutor Sir Thomas More, and venerable John Fisher, Bishop of Rochester. They accepted the order of succession included in the act but refused to take an oath to support the other provisions. In both cases, the decision was made with full knowledge of the dangers involved. On the eve of his indiscretion, More had been earnestly warned by his friend the Duke of Norfolk, who used an old Latin motto for the purpose. Said the duke, "It is perilous striving with princes, and I would wish you somewhat to incline to the King's pleasure, for, by God's body, Mr. More, *indignatio principis mors est* (the anger of a prince is death)."

More was an honest man with high ideals which he would not betray. Said he, "Is that all, my Lord? Is there, in good faith, no more difference between Your Grace and me but that I shall die today and you tomorrow?"

As soon as More's and Fisher's refusals became known, King Henry had them confined to the Tower, but there was to be more than a year of imprisonment before specific charges were brought.

Meanwhile, certain people of humbler stature but of equally high moral principles were meeting punishment through the enforcement of a law against heresy enacted by Henry's government. Henry's new heresy law permitted attacks upon the Pope and his associates in Rome but provided death by burning for all who should fail to assent to the religious decisions and beliefs of King Henry and his churchmen. Among those to suffer under this law were fourteen Anabaptists who had fled to England from Holland under the misconception that Henry would protect them because both he and they were opposed to some of Rome's beliefs. They were burned at the stake to demonstrate that Henry was a good Catholic except in cases in which the Pope's church differed from his own beliefs or opposed things he wished to do. Even more distressing was the execution of five priors of the monastery of Charterhouse in London (Carthusians) who remained completely loyal to the Roman Catholic Church and expressed their loyalty by repeating the Pope's decisions that Henry's marriage to Catherine was fully legal and that his marriage to Anne was not. One by one, they were drawn and quartered. As each man was treated in this way, those awaiting punishment were given a chance to change their opinions and thereby escape the horrible death ahead. No one would do so. All died for their faith.

Elizabeth Barton was a poor, uneducated servant girl who lived in Aldington, in the county of Kent. Like others in England, she had heard much of King Henry's campaign to divorce Catherine of Aragon and marry Anne Boleyn. In the summer of 1533, Elizabeth Barton fell ill and went through a long period of fever, delirium, and raving. Much of what she said made no sense at all, but some of it made altogether too much sense for her own good and the good of others. She said she saw a little devil whispering evil advice to Anne Boleyn, that she saw fiends snatching at the soul of Cardinal Wolsey after his death, that she saw the faces of the people who would be present when she should suffer martyrdom, that the spirits had told her that King Henry would not live more than seven months after his marriage to Anne Boleyn, that she had been shown the place in hell where the King would go when he had died a villain's death, and much more.

As word of "the divine revelations of the Holy Maid of Kent" spread, many prominent people went to see her and to question her. Archbishop Warham believed her divinely inspired and used his influence to get her to become a nun. Bishop Fisher and Sir Thomas More were among those who came and listened. Both were prisoners in the Tower before word of Elizabeth Barton's ravings reached the court.

Early in 1534, Elizabeth Barton was summoned to appear before Archbishop Cranmer at Canterbury, to tell about her "revelations" and to answer questions concerning them. Flattered, and more than anxious to help so important a man, she told her story, repeating the things she had said and supplying the names of people who had heard her say them. The complete record was sent to Thomas Cromwell.

Cromwell appreciated at once the opportunities offered him by the case of Elizabeth Barton. This girl had uttered treasonous predictions concerning His Majesty, the King, but no one who had heard her had reported the facts to King Henry. To withhold such vital information was nothing less than treason! Cromwell decided to use the information as a weapon to eliminate people who had been standing in the way of some cherished projects. People were questioned, notes were made, and the matter was laid before the king. Very shortly, an act of attainder was issued, bearing the names of Elizabeth Barton, Bishop Fisher, Sir Thomas More, the parson of the church at Aldington, and four less conspicuous persons. All were questioned, and seven of the eight were condemned to death. The one not condemned was Sir Thomas More. He had been able to establish, during the questioning, that his only contact with "the Holy Maid" had been to advise her not to say anything political or anything which concerned the king—advice to which she paid no attention whatsoever.

When Sir Thomas More was released, he was met by his devoted daughter Margaret, who was overflowing with joyful congratulations. There was no joy in his heart and no smiles on his face as he stilled her with one of his famed Latin quotations: "In faith, Meg, *quod differtur non aufertur*—what is postponed is not abandoned." Sir Thomas knew Cromwell and knew the king, so he was sure that there would be other moves against him.

The other seven who were indicted were condemned to death. Elizabeth Barton was to be burned at the stake, apparently with some thought that she had been tainted by witchcraft. The others were condemned to die under the headman's axe.

Whatever hope there had been for saving Bishop Fisher's life disappeared when the newly elected Pope Paul III made an ill-guided attempt to save him. Feeling that no one would presume to execute a cardinal of the Church, the pope appointed Bishop John Fisher to that position shortly before the time set for his execution. He had reckoned without headstrong King Henry. The seven executions were carried out as planned. When the axe had fallen on Bishop Fisher, the king exclaimed, with grisly humor, "Now his head may, if it can, go to Rome to get its Cardinal's hat."

Paul III, thoroughly outraged, promptly excommunicated King Henry. Any other Christian monarch would have been horrified and would have hastened to obey, but King Henry had gone so far in his break with the Church that this move by the new Pope offered little terror. Its sole effect was to widen the breach which had already developed between the Church of Rome and that of England.

As Sir Thomas More had told his daughter, postponement of

Sir Thomas More. (Portrait, 1527, by Hans Holbein the Younger)

the case against him did not mean its abandonment. He continued to insist that Parliament had no right to usurp the authority of the Pope, as the body was doing by making King Henry the head of the Church in England. He consistently refused to take the Oath of Supremacy, which would have meant that he supported the King as England's supreme churchman. Even worse, from King Henry's point of view, was More's refusal to admit the validity of the king's divorce from Catherine of Aragon. Many of King Henry's leading churchmen and intellectuals came to question Sir Thomas More and to argue with him. His nimble mind confounded all of them, with the possible exception of Archbishop Thomas Cranmer, concerning whom it was said that he could detect differences in meaning not visible to ordinary human eyes.

At last, the game played out. The questioners tired of trying to entrap their brilliant quarry and brought against him a simple charge of treason for opposing the grant of full religious authority to King Henry. More was found guilty and was condemned to die by decapitation. As he was being led to the Tower, his faithful daughter twice forced her way through the ranks of the guards to kiss him good-bye.

As the day of the execution approached, Sir Thomas More received a final note from the king he had served so well. It was only a single sentence, asking that "at your execution you shall not use many words."

The words, as requested, were few. As he started to climb the scaffold, it swayed beneath his weight, threatening to collapse. Turning to Sir William Kingston, Constable of the Tower, he said with a smile, "I pray thee, see me safe up. For my coming down, I can shift for myself." He had already presented the executioner with a gold coin "for services to be rendered." Now, as he knelt beside the block, he said to the man with the axe, "Thou art to do me the greatest benefit I can receive. Pluck up thy spirit, man, and be not afraid to do thine office. My neck is very short. Take heed, therefore, that thou strike not awry, for the saving of thine honesty." Then he laid his head on the block, but before the headsman could swing his axe he raised up again, gathered up his beard, which had grown long during his imprisonment, and carefully arranged it beyond the block. As he did so, he spoke his final words: "Pity that should be cut that has not committed treason."

The head of Sir Thomas More was impaled on a spike on London Bridge, but it did not remain there long. Under cover of darkness, his daughter Meg went onto the bridge and stole her father's head, keeping it safely hidden during her lifetime and having it buried in her arms when she died.

# 8
# QUEEN ANNE BOLEYN

ONE might well have thought, as Anne Boleyn, indeed, did, that the death of Queen Catherine would bring complete happiness to her rival and successor. It was a tremendous shock to the new queen to discover that the results were precisely opposite.

As long as there had been a divorce to seek and a rival to flaunt, the king had taken delight in lavishing his favors on Anne. With Catherine's death, Henry could see much less reason to heap honors on his new queen.

A distressing truth slowly forced its way into the mind of Anne Boleyn. King Henry was not a man who could stay long in love with any one woman, nor could he be faithful to his wife, no matter who she might be.

Word reached Queen Anne that Henry was having an affair with one of the ladies of the court, whose name is not known. Feeling her position to be in danger, Anne decided to announce that she was pregnant, for she was sure that the king would not turn against her while she might be carrying the legitimate son which he so greatly wanted. Her announcement had the desired effect. Henry ceased his attentions to the lady and returned to honoring his wife. Unfortunately, though, her deception could not be carried on for long. Before many weeks, she had to tell the king that she had been mistaken and was not pregnant after all. He became bitter and returned to his affair with the unnamed lady.

Anne Boleyn, Henry's second wife. (Portrait by an unknown artist)

Anne's next bit of strategy backfired badly. The king's mistress was intensely opposed to the queen and missed no opportunity to attack her. The girl must go, even if she was immediately replaced by another. The help of the Boleyn family was secured, and through their influence Margaret Shelton was brought to court. As hoped, King Henry found her most attractive and she became his mistress. Margaret was friendly to Anne, but it was still unpleasant to have another woman in the king's bed.

Despite King Henry's current preference for other women and his repeated statements to his intimate friends that he wanted to have no more to do with Anne, she apparently did receive an occasional invitation to visit him for a night. She was still his wife and queen and represented the only chance he could see for having the legitimate son and heir he so desperately needed.

In time, hope raised its head. Queen Anne became pregnant. The king was delighted and Lady Shelton soon found herself without her lover.

King Henry, though, was not quite ready to be a completely faithful husband, even though Queen Anne might be carrying his longed-for son and heir. The sprightly qualities, which originally had attacted him to Anne, now seemed to repel him— the lighthearted playfulness, the tendency to laugh immoderately at anything and nothing, and, most of all, the flirtatiousness, directed at any courtier who paid attention to her.

It was in that frame of mind that King Henry made one of his customary "progresses" through the kingdom and stopped at Wolf Hall, a manor house in Wiltshire. There he met Lady Jane Seymour, the quiet and virtuous daughter of his old friend Sir John Seymour, who had been with him at the Field of the Cloth of Gold. By ordinary standards, Jane Seymour was not beautiful, but her manner captivated the king. Her modest quietness was in sharp contrast to Queen Anne's noisy and sense-less-seeming laughter, and her modest behavior no one could doubt. When he offered her gifts of great value, she returned them unopened, saying that such gifts might come better at a time when he was free to give and she to accept them.

It was during her fourth month of pregnancy that Queen Anne Boleyn's world began to collapse. One day in mid-January 1536, she casually entered the king's chamber and was amazed to see Jane Seymour sitting on Henry's lap. Queen Anne knew Jane Seymour as a demure lady of the court, but so discreet had the two lovers been that this was her first intimation that there was anything between them. The shock was great, causing Anne to burst out with an indignant tirade of abuse. Henry, fearful that in her hysterical state she might miscarry his son and heir, tried to quiet her, but his efforts were in vain.

Not many days afterward, King Henry took part in a tournament. As he came riding down the course, clad in full armor, his opponent's lance caught him at an awkward angle, throwing him to the ground and upsetting his armored war-horse so that it fell upon him. First reports said the king was dead, but after several hours he was brought back to consciousness, and it was found that he was not so badly injured as had first been supposed.

The shock of these two events had just the effect that both King Henry and Queen Anne had feared. On January 29, 1536 —five days after King Henry's jousting accident—the queen gave premature birth to a dead baby boy.

Completely disregarding the frightful physical experience his wife had just had and the even more grievous blow of losing the baby boy who had been expected to mean so much to both of them, he stormed into Anne's chamber and cursed her for having lost *his* son. As he was leaving the room, he turned back and shouted, "You shall have no other sons by me!"

As King Henry had indicated, he no longer went to Queen Anne's chambers nor invited her to his. His time was spent with Jane Seymour, in anticipation of the time when he would be free to make her his queen. Queen Anne spent much of her time alone. She no longer had Princess Elizabeth with her, for the little girl was being raised by others, to prevent her mother from turning her against the king. In this sad time, the only comfort came from Anne's sister Mary, who overcame her differences with Anne in order to be with her.

Anne Boleyn's troubles began when Eustace Chapuys appeared in England as an ambassador from Emperor Charles V. Now that Queen Catherine was dead, there was less to prevent friendly relations between the ruler of the Holy Roman Empire and the King of England than there had been when the king had been trying to divorce the emperor's aunt. Cromwell was very anxious to bring increased peace and understanding between the governments, but King Henry would not cooperate. The king could not be moved in his opposition—an opposition which Cromwell believed had had its origin in Anne Boleyn's rivalry with the emperor's aunt, Catherine of Aragon. The evidence seemed to indicate that Queen Anne's influence was still strong in that area. Now that the king and queen had had their difficulties, Cromwell decided it might be the time to rid England of this troublesome lady.

Among Queen Anne's attendants was a talented young musician named Mark Smeaton. During the lonely period when the king had been neglecting her, Smeaton brought her some pleasure by playing on his lute. Cromwell invited the young man to his home. Smeaton went, expecting good food and enjoyment, but what he found was stern questioning by the great official and torture at the hands of two of Cromwell's henchmen, who bound his head with a rope and twisted it tighter and tighter with a stout cudgel until his assertions of innocence gave way to confessions of anything that Cromwell desired and any names that he wanted to hear. Smeaton was taken upstairs and locked in a room of Cromwell's house. He had implicated not only himself but also a number of other men whose names he had blurted out as the rope had drawn tighter and tighter about his skull.

The next day, May 1, was the date for the great May Day Tournament at Greenwich. King Henry had been unable to compete in tournaments since his accident some months before, but he attended as the most honored of spectators. Queen Anne was there, too, for her brother George, Viscount Rochford, was one of the two principal contenders, the other being King Henry's close friend of many years Sir Henry Norris. The king, having just been told by Cromwell the results of Smeaton's questioning, was hurt and in an ugly mood. The queen, knowing nothing of this, was prepared to enjoy one of the few and rare outings since the loss of her son. The royal couple, with a number of friends and attendants, occupied a raised box overlooking the jousting lists.

Between two jousts, Sir Henry Norris paused beneath the royal box. Queen Anne held in her hand a kerchief which, either by accident or on purpose, she let fall. It landed at Norris's feet, and he picked it up. Accounts differ about whether he kissed it or wiped his face with it, but whatever he did, it startled King Henry. Norris was one of those mentioned by Mark Smeaton. The king rose and left the box, accompanied by six of his friends. Before leaving the grounds, he summoned Norris to ride back to the castle with him.

The king and Norris rode apart from the others, talking in low voices as King Henry told his lifelong friend of the evidence uncovered by Cromwell and urged him to save his own life by pleading guilty and telling all he knew of the queen's other affairs. Norris was horrified. He refused to admit anything, asserting that he was innocent and that he knew nothing of any love affairs between Queen Anne and anybody else. He was locked up in the Tower to await trial.

The next day, Queen Anne was being served her noontime

dinner. Every day, the king's own waiter had appeared at her table with the main course and a goodwill message from her husband: "Much good may it do you." This time, he did not appear, but she had scarcely had time to feel a sense of foreboding when others appeared with a message expressing anything but goodwill: "Prepare yourself! We have come to take you to the Tower by barge." The servants had known sometime before. A number of them had been weeping as they began to serve the meal.

Before being taken out to the barge, Queen Anne was severely questioned by her estranged uncle, the Duke of Norfolk. She was told that Norris and Smeaton had confessed to adultery with her. Shocked and terrified, she tried to deny any wrongdoing, but each time she opened her mouth to speak, her uncle indicated his disbelief by overriding comments of "Tut! Tut! *Tut!!*" At last, failing to get a confession, the questioners took her to the barge. She was rowed upstream to the Tower in the custody of her Uncle Norfolk, two court chamberlains, and a guard.

At the water gate to the Tower stood the constable, Sir William Kingston, who had greeted her three years before when she had first arrived as the new queen. "Master Kingston," she quavered, "do I go into a dungeon?"

"No, madam. You shall go into the lodging where you lay at your coronation."

The bitter contrast hit her hard. Tears burst from her eyes, and she sobbed. Then, suddenly, she was laughing—high, hysterical laughter that for some time she could not control.

When she regained her self-control, she asked why she had been brought to the Tower. Kingston told her that she had been charged with misconduct with four men, adding the names of Sir Francis Weston and William Brereton to the two she already knew—Norris and Smeaton. Vehemently, she protested her innocence. Turning again to the constable, she asked, "Master Kingston, shall I die without justice?"

With all apparent sincerity, he gravely replied, "The poorest subject of the King hath justice."

She asked for her brother, Sir George Boleyn, Viscount Rochford. Constable Kingston evaded an honest answer this time, saying that he had last seen George Boleyn at York Place. It was true that he had seen him there no later than that morning, for he had gone to York Place to arrest him on the most degrading charge of all—incest with his own sister. Kingston had not the heart to tell her this.

A sixth man was arrested soon after the others. He was a famous poet, Sir Thomas Wyatt, Queen Anne's first cousin. Before Anne had become queen, Wyatt had pursued her and had recorded the pursuit in a poem which (with spelling and grammar modernized and an English phrase in place of a Latin one) went as follows:

> He who wishes to hunt: I know where is a hind,
>   But, as for me, alas I may no more.
>   The vain travail has wearied me so sore
> I am of them that farthest come behind.
> Yet, may I, by no means, my wearied mind
>   Draw from the deer; but as she flees before,
>   Fainting I follow. I leave off therefore,
> Since in a net I seek to hold the wind.
> Who wishes to hunt her: I put him out of doubt.
>   As well as I, he'll spend his time in vain,
>   For, graven with diamonds in letters plain,
> There is written, her fair neck roundabout:
>   "Do not touch me, for Caesar's I am
>   And wild to hold, though I seem tame."

Yes, she was "Caesar's," and it was well for Wyatt that he had realized that early. No evidence was produced against him, and after some weeks of harried imprisonment he was released.

The other defendants did not fare so well. Norris, who had

been King Henry's best friend and the only courtier admitted to his bedroom as he undressed, did not even deign to honor the ridiculous charges by any defense at all, other than a matter-of-fact statement that he was not guilty. Weston, Brereton, and Anne's brother George, Viscount Rochford, also pleaded not guilty and attempted to prove their innocence. The attempt was made in vain. All three were declared guilty and condemned to death, though the evidence against Rochford was extremely feeble, consisting merely of testimony that the brother and sister had once been alone together for several hours. Smeaton, having already pleaded guilty under torture, knew that his case was hopeless and made no effort to change his plea or to plead that he was innocent. When the death sentences had been pronounced, not one of the five criticized the trial they had received.

All of the defendants and, in fact, everyone connected with the trial knew that King Henry and Thomas Cromwell had decided upon guilty verdicts for all accused. Cromwell had convinced the king that all five defendants were guilty and that in cuckolding and disgracing their king they had performed acts of gross treason. Henry was consumed with rage and inspired to demand complete and dreadful punishment of all concerned. In this situation, no jury would have dared find the accused men innocent. But there was no protest. Each of the five was well aware of the custom, then prevalent, of inflicting heavy penalties on the families of men condemned to death who wrote or uttered statements harmful or embarrassing to those who had found them guilty. To protect their families, they had to remain silent, even in the face of death.

On May 17, 1536—five days after their trial—the five men were led into the Tower courtyard under the windows of Queen Anne's prison quarters and put to death—four under the headsman's axe and the fifth, Smeaton, by hanging, because he was a commoner. There is some evidence that Smeaton had been quietly promised his life if he would repeat his earlier confession of guilt. If so, he was betrayed, for his repeated confession was followed by his execution. Before kneeling and laying their heads on the block, Weston, Brereton, and Rochford made brief statements that they were not guilty. Norris died with the most dignity of all, refusing to say anything concerning the ridiculous proceedings which were costing him his life. Whether or not any of the others were guilty as charged, it seems evident that he, at least, had been completely innocent.

On May 18, Anne Boleyn was visited by Archbishop Cranmer, who asked her many questions and led her to believe that she was not to be executed after all.

In reality, Archbishop Cranmer was on a special assignment from King Henry. What he sought from her was definite assurance, in as much detail as possible, that her sister Mary had been King Henry's mistress before he had married Anne Boleyn. Hope had been given her, largely for the purpose of getting her to talk. With the information secured, Cranmer retired to work up a divorce case, based on much the same grounds as the earlier case which had pried Catherine of Aragon loose from Henry. The same passage from Leviticus was quoted, but this time it was stretched to cover the case of a man whose wife's sister had been his mistress before the marriage. The Roman Catholic Church had previously turned this down as grounds for divorce, but the king and the English Church were no longer under the authority of the Pope. There was nothing to prevent Thomas Cranmer, Archbishop of Canterbury, from declaring the divorce official on these or any other grounds he wished, since he was now the highest-ranking churchman in England.

Anne's hopes quickly vanished, now that Cranmer had the information he required. When she learned that she was to lose her head, she requested that the decapitation be done by an expert swordsman, such as those who carried out executions in the court of France, rather than an English headsman wielding an axe. The request was granted, and a swordsman was brought across the channel from Calais.

On her final day—May 19, 1536—Queen Anne Boleyn had herself remarkably well under control and seemed unnaturally cheerful. She had originally expected to die soon after sunrise, but the execution was postponed for half a day. When the constable made his final visit to her, she repeated her earlier protestations of innocence, then added, "Mr. Kingston, I hear that I am not to die before noon, and I am very sorry for it, for I thought to be dead and past my pain."

He assured her that it would happen so fast that there would be no pain.

Queen Anne put her long fingers around her neck. Said she, "I heard say that the executioner from Calais is more expert than any in England. That is very good. I have a *little* neck."

When the time came, Queen Anne made a quiet little speech, forgiving the king for what was being done to her and calling upon the witnesses to pray for him. Then she donned a linen cap over her hair, permitted her eyes to be bandaged, and placed her head upon the block.

# 9
# JANE SEYMOUR

O N the day following Anne Boleyn's execution, Henry and Jane Seymour were betrothed. Ten days later, they were married in a quiet and unspectacular ceremony in the queen's "closet"—an old term for private sitting room—at York Place. This was the same room in which he had married Anne Boleyn a little over three years before.

It would be hard to imagine three women more different from one another than King Henry's first three wives. Catherine of Aragon had been devoted, serious, and fanatically Catholic. To the day of her death, she had been deeply in love with Henry. Had she been younger than her husband, rather than older, and had she been able to produce a living son, she might have been the one and perfect Queen of his reign. Anne was pleasure bent —her motto was "me and mine"—cursed with a complete lack of judgment and fitness, and altogether too fond of flirtation. If she had borne a living boy and if she had displayed even a minimum of prudence, she might have been Henry's final wife.

Jane Seymour was quiet; modest; timid; with a great love for and fear of King Henry; and with an intention to do everything in her power to make him happy and to make his reign a success. Her motto contrasts well with Anne's; it was "Bound to Obey and Serve."

Very shortly after the wedding, rumor spread that Queen Jane was pregnant. Indeed, the question has been seriously raised

Jane Seymour, Henry's third wife. (Portrait by an unknown artist)

by historians whether she was not pregnant before the wedding; whether it was not this fact which caused the quick trial and almost immediate execution of Queen Anne Boleyn, rather than the longer procedure of seeking a divorce and thus losing the opportunity to claim an heir legitimately conceived and born in wedlock. It was not the shame of having an illegitimate child that mattered. The king's bastard son, Henry Fitzroy, was evidence that this was not too serious an act. It was, rather, the absolute necessity of having a legitimate heir because Elizabeth had been made illegitimate by King Henry's divorce from Queen Anne Boleyn. It was up to Queen Jane to produce one or more sons as quickly as possible. Unfortunately, the initial rumor proved to be false.

There was hope that the royal pair would conceive children in the months and years ahead, hope that was to be thoroughly realized in the following spring when the queen was discovered to be officially and unquestionably pregnant.

Though the birth of a prince was the overriding purpose of Jane Seymour's life as Henry's queen, she had another aim almost as dear. Henry's elder daughter, Mary, had been living in seclusion and neglect ever since the divorce of her mother, Catherine of Aragon. She was now twenty years old, but looked much older, for her expression was bleak, her face pinched and pursed, her complexion gray. Not without good reason did she feel that her mother had been shamefully treated in being summarily divorced and deprived of husband, title, and honors. Even more did she resent the break with the Church and the denial of the Pope's authority. She was a rigid and devout Roman Catholic, with no use or tolerance for the new and convenient deviations which her father and his associates were creating. To Jane Seymour, it appeared that it would be most worthwhile to work for a reconciliation between King Henry and his estranged daughter, Princess Mary.

When first approached on the matter, King Henry seemed receptive. Then, as so often happened, the king changed his mind. There were many at court who hoped for the best even while they were counting on the worst. Men who had faithfully served Henry in many ways—even Cromwell—were not in sympathy with him in the hard line he had taken toward his daughter. The king knew this, but there was no room in England for anyone who would not admit his complete dominance.

A three-man delegation was sent to call upon Princess Mary and obtain her submission. Richard Sampson, Bishop of Chichester, was one member; the others were the Dukes of Norfolk and Sussex. When they had told her what was expected of her, she was horrified. As much as she wanted to be reconciled with her father, she was not ready to sign a paper stating that her mother's marriage was illegal and incestuous, that she herself was a bastard, and that the Pope had no spiritual or legal rights over the Church in England. The three men argued, pleaded, and threatened, but it did little good.

Eustace Chapuys, the ambassador from the Holy Roman Empire, had been keeping a careful eye on the situation and had been sending frequent dispatches to Emperor Charles V, who was very concerned. As Queen Catherine had been Charles's aunt, Princess Mary was his cousin. Through Chapuys, he sent her his advice—that she submit entirely, even though she had to lie to do it, "for God regards more the intention than the act."

Princess Mary tried. She wrote a submissive letter and sent it to Cromwell, to give to the king. Cromwell did so, though he could see that the letter did not go nearly far enough in self-abasement. King Henry was furious.

Thomas Cromwell had originally interested himself in Princess Mary's case, not out of friendship or humanitarian feelings but because he had felt that if the two princesses should be restored to favor they would eventually be used in marriages to foreign princes, to the advantage of England, of King Henry, and himself. Now the matter was out of hand and he wrote the princess, calling upon her for complete humbleness and submission, without any reservations, any mentions of God or her conscience. He called her the most obstinate and obdurate of women. "I am ashamed," he wrote. "I am afraid. . . . If you will not with speed leave off all your sinister counsels, which have brought you to the point of utter undoing without remedy, I take my leave of you forever and desire you to write to me no more, for I will never think you other than the most ungrateful, unnatural, and obstinate person living, both to God and your most dear and benign father." To make sure that she knew exactly what he meant, Cromwell included with his letter a masterpiece of literary groveling, a sample letter that left no shred or tatter of the writer's self-regard.

Princess Mary understood. She sat down at once, and copied Cromwell's letter word for word in her own handwriting: "Most humbly prostrate before the feet of your most excellent Majesty, your most humble, faithful, and obedient subject which hath so extremely offended your most gracious Highness that mine heavy and fearful heart dare not presume to call you father." It went on and on in this vein, speaking of the king as "merciful, compassionate, most blessed, . . . Supreme Head of the Church." She spoke of the Pope as a pretender and of her mother's marriage as "by God's law and man's law, incestuous and unlawful."

The king tentatively accepted it, though he did require her soon afterward to appear before him and his Council and repeat the same sentiments in person. She did so.

Only very gradually did Princess Mary realize how very near the edge of the precipice she had been. Very gradually and grudgingly, King Henry brought her back into the family. Little by little, the tension gave way. Queen Jane gave her a valuable

diamond as a sign of affection, and the king bestowed upon
her a considerable sum of money "for your little pleasures."
She was given the care of her three-year-old half sister Elizabeth,
and both girls came to the royal court to live. Queen Jane had
magnificently achieved her worthy purpose.

Henry's Queen was pregnant but the royal succession was still
anything but settled. All three of his present children were illegitimate, Henry Fitzroy naturally so, Mary and Elizabeth legally.
Parliament was summoned, listened to its master's voice, and
passed an extraordinary act of succession. By the terms of this
new law, legitimate male offspring of King Henry and Jane
Seymour or some other future queen of his were to succeed to
the throne, in order of age. If there were no such heirs, the
throne was to go to whomever King Henry should designate,
either in person or by a written message left behind at his
death.

Apparently, King Henry had decided that, failing the birth
of new and legitimate heirs, he would leave the throne to Henry
Fitzroy, Princess Mary, and Princess Elizabeth, in that order.
Fate quickly intervened. Henry Fitzroy, never very strong, had
been dying ever since the execution of Queen Anne Boleyn, which
he had been compelled to witness. He died on July 24, 1536, of a
lung infection, leaving King Henry with no male offspring, legitimate or illegitimate.

King Henry had a cousin, Reginald Pole, who was an ardent
churchman with an amazing ability to escape unscathed after
saying or doing rash things. Born in 1500, he was nine years
younger than Henry, who had paid for his education and paid
him a royal pension of 500 crowns a year. One would have
thought that such a man would be one of the staunchest cham-
pions of the emerging Church of England. In fact, he was anything but that.

The first sign of disagreement came when Henry was seeking

his divorce from Catherine of Aragon and asked Cousin Reginald for his opinion. Pole answered that he could not approve it unless it were first sanctioned by the Pope, which it was not. To further demonstrate his disapproval, he then refused an appointment as Archbishop of York in order to return to the Continent to continue his studies. Henry permitted him to go and even continued to pay him his pension.

In 1536, Reginald Pole became a cardinal of the Roman Catholic Church. He celebrated the event by attacking King Henry and his English Church. His book—*Pro Ecclesiasticae Unitatis Defensione (In Defense of Church Unity)*—struck hard at King Henry's new Church. Concerning Henry, himself, he said, among many other things, "During the twenty-seven years he has reigned, he has continually plundered his subjects, and, if he was liberal in anything, it was certainly not in the things that make for the common weal. He has robbed every kind of man, made sport of the nobility, never loved the people, troubled the clergy, and torn like a wild beast the men who were the greatest honor to his kingdom." He compared King Henry to such Roman tyrants as Nero and Domitian. With some justice, he criticized the English churchmen for permitting Henry to divide the Church. He called upon Charles V, who was currently carrying out a military expedition against a Mediterranean pirate named Barbarossa, to stop shooting at Mohammedans and to save his ammunition for use against King Henry's England.

Strangely enough, Cardinal Pole did not expect King Henry to be upset by the attack. He seemed to think that King Henry would be grateful to Pole for pointing out his mistakes.

King Henry indicated that he was not disturbed by what the cardinal had written and invited him to come to England and discuss the matter.

Fortunately for Cardinal Pole, there were others who were more difficult to deceive. The alert Chapuys wrote the emperor that King Henry wanted to execute this cardinal, just as he had executed Cardinal John Fisher. Pole's friends and family warned him, so that he did not go to England.

Henry was furious and hastened his seizure and liquidation of the Roman Catholic monasteries in England.

Early in October 1536, word reached King Henry that the common people from the northern counties of Lincolnshire and Yorkshire were angry over what was happening to the Church that had for so long meant so much to them. A few of the local nobles and Church officials voluntarily joined the cause; many others were forced to join. Their leader was an earnest attorney named Robert Aske. Among the others were Abbot Makerel of Barlings (known to his followers as Captain Cobbler); Lords Darcy, Nevil, Latimer, and Lumley; two of the famous fighting Percy family; and others. A complicated banner was adopted, including pictures of a plow, a chalice, a horn, and the five wounds of Jesus on the cross. The name of the campaign was the Pilgrimage of Grace.

Since King Henry had almost no troops mustered and under arms with which to oppose the estimated twenty thousand armed and indignant countrymen, he preferred to negotiate. Emissaries were received who bore lists of demands. Henry studied the lists, learning from them that the members of the Pilgrimage were not intent upon civil war but wanted the adoption of certain reforms: the restoration of the monasteries, the easing of taxes, the discontinuing of certain payments being extracted by the government from the clergy, the elimination of "villein blood" (meaning Thomas Cromwell) from the King's Privy Council, and the discharge and punishment of "heretic bishops" (meaning Cranmer and Latimer). There was no doubting the serious purpose back of the movement. Two of Cromwell's agents, who had been caught carrying out their assignments of liquidating monasteries, had been killed. Shortly afterward, Aske's army took York and Pomfret and another group of the Pilgrims captured Hull.

Word from abroad increased King Henry's worries. Pope Paul III and Cardinal Reginald Pole were using all of their influence to convince King Francis I of France and Emperor Charles V to abandon their own quarrels, unite their forces, and overthrow King Henry and his "wicked and heretical" government. They would never have a better chance, as King Henry knew all too well.

Still, trying to gain time for military preparation, King Henry sent a small force north under the Duke of Norfolk, while he himself devoted his full attention to raising and equipping all the fighting men he could. To put the rebels off guard, he sent word to Robert Aske that the king was interested in the Pilgrims' demands and would like to meet the leader of the movement. The attorney hastened south to London, counting fully on the king's promise of safe-conduct.

King Henry assumed his most charming and disarming manner, seeming to give full attention to everything that Aske told him and indicating substantial agreement. At the same time, the Duke of Norfolk, far to the north, was also feigning agreement and promising complete pardon for everyone who had taken part in the pilgrimage. The wrongs would be righted, and justice would be done. Men who had been ready to give their lives could see no point in staying away from home.

Queen Jane Seymour could not help but become aware of what her husband and his advisors had in mind. With utter disregard for any personal danger, she implored the king to restore the abbeys and monasteries, saying that the rebellion in the north was God's punishment for their liquidation. The king was outraged. When she strove to continue her protests, he reminded her of what had happened to Anne Boleyn. Weeping, she fled.

The Duke of Norfolk, following King Henry's orders, was

looking for an excuse, any excuse, to repudiate the oral agreement that had been made with Robert Aske. As Aske was returning to the north country, bearing a red satin jacket which the king had given him in place of the written guarantees that Aske had wanted, the duke found his excuse. Two minor leaders of the rebellion, Bigod and Hallam, conducted a raid without Aske's knowledge or consent. The duke had with him definite instructions from King Henry, opening with these words: "Our pleasure is that before you close up our banner again you shall cause such dreadful execution to be done upon a good number of the inhabitants of every town, village, and hamlet that have offended, that they may be a fearful spectacle to all others hereafter that would practice any like matter. . . ."

The duke carried out his orders. Hundreds of those who had taken part in the pilgrimage were put to death, religious houses looted and their inhabitants scattered without shelter or source of income. Cromwell prospered greatly by accepting bribes offered by those hoping to save some particular shrine or abbey; though the money was taken, the destruction was carried out.

Following many weeks of intensive questioning, the leaders were executed.

Robert Aske remained calm and unembittered, concerned that his creditors, friends, and family be well treated. For himself, he asked, "Let me be full dead ere I be dismembered." He got his wish. He was hanged. Others were far more cruelly treated. In Lincolnshire, some of the original leaders were hanged, drawn, and quartered.

Lord Darcy, facing his own death by the axe, had an opportunity to utter a telling and prophetic comment. Cromwell was present at his execution, and to Cromwell he laid most of the blame for the executions that were taking place. His final words, addressed directly to Cromwell, were, "Yet, shall there one head remain, that shall strike off *thy* head!"

Now that the Pilgrimage of Grace had been utterly crushed, King Henry felt free to relax and to await the birth of his child. Much of his time was spent in the queen's presence.

One of the frequent subjects of discussion between the king and the queen was what name to bestow upon their expected son. Should he be called Henry or Edward? The child himself settled the matter. Queen Jane's time of delivery came on October 11, 1537, but the baby refused to emerge. For thirty hours, Queen Jane suffered the agonies of arrested childbirth, while the king, the doctors, and the attendants hovered anxiously over her. A baby boy was born by Caesarian section, October 12. This was an important religious date—the anniversary of the vigil of St. Edward. Without further discussion, the little prince was named Edward.

The baptism itself occurred on the third day after the birth. The Archbishop of Canterbury presided, and the guests included virtually everyone in the court. Unfortunately, Queen Jane, who should have been in bed, was among them. She caught a serious cold, and nine days later she was dead.

# 10
# THE GREAT FLEMISH MARE

KING Henry was genuinely distressed by the death of Queen Jane. He retired from public view, wishing only to be alone. Though he intensely disliked the color black, he promptly donned mourning clothes and wore them exclusively during the forty-day period. It seems evident that he had loved Jane Seymour more deeply than anyone else, except for Prince Edward.

For the time being, King Henry was not interested in acquiring another wife. This, though, did not prevent Thomas Cromwell from making quiet inquiries concerning available marriage partners in whom the king might later be interested. The line of succession was still not well anchored, for Prince Edward was not particularly robust or healthy. Another two or three princes, waiting in succession, would make things far more secure.

Even more imminent was the problem of securing allies. The Pope was working hard to get King Francis of France and Emperor Charles V to break off their intermittent warfare and unite in a great Catholic crusade against the "heretic King of England." If King Henry could and would marry a member of one of those royal families, the prospective alliance against him would be rendered impossible and he would have a powerful ally of his own.

On the day Queen Jane died, Cromwell wrote to Lord William Howard in France, stating that "though His Majesty is not anything disposed to marry again," the members of his Council feel it important "that His Grace again couple himself." Howard was urged to render a report on "the conditions and qualities" of King Francis' daughter Margaret and of Mary of Guise, widow of the Duke de Longueville.

As weeks, then months, went by with the king in retirement and unseen by most of his subjects, the rumor began to spread that he had died. Though the possibility was suggested with real concern, and in most cases without any wishful thinking, even the mention of such a thing was considered by King and Council as unfriendly and somewhat treasonous. Many of the rumor-mongers were quietly arrested, and in every case the punishment was the same. Their ears were cut off. They were stripped naked. Their wrists were fastened together and tied to the tailboard of a cart, and they were whipped through the streets of the town in which they had spread their rumor.

Little by little, King Henry began to take a new interest in life and in his two principal activities—the continued formulation of his new Church and the search for a new queen to supply love, comfort, and—hopefully—several additional new heirs. It cannot be said that either of these interests was far ahead of the other in point of time, but the religious aspects bore the first important fruit.

Religiously, King Henry, Archbishops Cranmer and Latimer, and their associates in the Church of England were treading a narrow and slippery path between the Roman Catholic Church and Martin Luther's Protestant group. King Henry did not wish to be dictated to by the Pope and therefore insisted that he, rather than the Pope, was the supreme head and authority of the Church in England. Thomas Fuller, in his *Church History*, described him as "a king with a pope in his belly." The difference from Protestantism was much greater. King Henry and his associates were just as ready as the authorities in Rome to punish members of the Lutheran and other Protestant groups as heretics.

An important additional difference from Rome was the publication of the Bible in English. The Roman Church permitted only Latin versions of the Bible, which the clergy could read but few others could understand. This gave a magical, mystical aura to the holy word and to the dedicated men who could interpret it. As early as 1525, an Englishman named William Tyndale, living in Cologne, Germany, printed an English-language version of the New Testament. King Henry was not yet ready for this simplifying of Holy Writ, so he had Tyndale's Bible suppressed in England. In 1536 Tyndale himself was arrested in Antwerp and burned at the stake. The very next year, though, an English-language Bible translated by Miles Coverdale was accepted by the English government, and in 1538 Thomas Cromwell commissioned Coverdale to prepare an expanded edition. In 1540, Archbishop Cranmer and Coverdale collaborated to produce *The Great Bible*, which became the official holy book of King Henry's new Church of England.

The Lambert case illustrates clearly both King Henry's narrow path between religious extremes and his increasing activity in the field of religon. Lambert (whose real but seldom used name was John Nicholson) was a "sacramentarian"; that is, he believed and maintained that the bread and wine consumed in the communion service were not actually the flesh and blood of Jesus but merely represented them. Being on one of his swings toward the Roman Catholic point of view, King Henry announced that he would publicly debate with Lambert, convince him of his error, and silence him forever. The unfortunate man was sentenced to appear before his king and a panel of twelve high churchmen, headed by Archbishop Cranmer. King Henry appeared dressed all in white, which made him appear even larger and more impressive than he was. The king asked a few questions, which Lambert was too terrified to answer very coherently, though the general impression was that he had not changed his viewpoint. In closing, Henry reminded his victim of the statement which Jesus had made at the Last Supper: "This is my body." Lambert was then turned over to the churchmen, who questioned, heckled, and browbeat him for five hours, until he was utterly exhausted. The king's chief contribution was a severe and disapproving expression which never left his face.

At the conclusion of the debate, King Henry asked Lambert whether he had been convinced, a question which he either would not or could not answer. He then asked him if he wished to live or die.

Stammering and scarcely able to speak, Lambert finally managed to say, "I entrust my soul to God and my body to Your Grace's clemency."

"Well, then, you shall die. I am not in the habit of protecting heretics."

The panel approved the sentence, and Cromwell read the decision. A few days later, Lambert was burned at the stake, shouting, "None but Christ," until he was dead.

The Lambert case represented a person with a Catholic point of view striking at a Protestant doctrine. At approximately the same time, there were many examples of the same royal personage assuming a Protestant point of view to strike at Catholic beliefs. Conveniently, King Henry could assume whichever series of beliefs best suited his interests at any given moment.

As the monasteries, nunneries, shrines, abbeys, and other Catholic religious institutions were being liquidated, vast quantities of gold, jewels, and other precious items were turned over to King Henry or to his government. At the same time, other cherished items were taken which had little cash value but were said to have miraculous powers for curing the body and/or the soul. For countless generations, pilgrims had knelt before these relics, their hearts full of hope. King Henry did not believe these relics were genuine and he ordered most of them destroyed and a few exhibited as proofs of deceit by the clergy.

Some of the churchmen tried to preserve at least a part of their treasures by hiding them before the looters sent by King Henry and Cromwell could find and evaluate them. This soon proved to be an extremely dangerous activity, and a useless one, as well. The abbey at Glastonbury, for example, seemed to be yielding less wealth than had been expected. A thorough search was made and the missing treasures uncovered. Wrote one of the officials, in his report to Cromwell: "We have daily found and tried out both money and plate, hid and muried up in walls, vaults, and other secret places. . . . The abbot and the monks have embezzled and stolen as much plate and adornments as would have sufficed to have begun a new abbey." Abbot Whiting and two of his monks were promptly tried and convicted. The next day they were executed, "the said abbot's body being divided into four parts and head stricken off." Even the head was made to serve a useful purpose, for it was fastened to the abbey gate as a warning to others who might try the same sort of "embezzlement and theft."

If it seems strange that men should be charged with stealing articles which for hundreds of years remained in the same place, and were still under the guardianship of the men who had been officially placed in charge of them, one has only to look at the law which Parliament passed in 1539 at the demand of the king and Cromwell. This law—"An Act for the Dissolution of Abbeys"—made legal the looting of the Church properties, which was already well under way. Church valuables and lands were sold to the highest bidder in order to support King Henry's luxurious court and his wars.

The year 1539 was very active for new laws connected with religion. The law concerning abbeys was soon followed by "An

Act for the King to Make Bishops," and that by one providing for the seizing and abolition of chantries, which were Church organizations that accepted gifts and donations and offered in return prayers for the souls of people who had died. In July came the most sweeping religious act of all, "An Act Abolishing the Diversity in Opinions," also known as "The Act of the Six Articles" by its supporters and "The Whip with Six Strings" by nearly everyone else. It listed six specific beliefs that everyone was required to hold: that the blood and flesh of Jesus were really present in the Eucharist; that all churchmen must be celibate; that monks must live up to the vows which they had made when entering their order; that masses, both public and private, might be said for the souls of the dead; that either of the two forms of communion was acceptable and sufficient; and that confession must be made regularly and aloud to a priest, in privacy. People convicted of violating the first of the six articles were burned to death, and those violating any of the other five articles were fined and imprisoned for a first offense and executed for a second.

Even the top clergymen were not excused. Archbishop Cranmer, who had been secretly married to a German girl and had quietly brought his bride to England, quickly sent her back to the Continent to avoid prosecution. Bishops Latimer and Shaxton were both imprisoned for speaking out against some of the six provisions. Although it was stated that the purpose of the law was more to frighten and to silence dissenters than to punish them, some twenty-eight were put to death under its provisions and many hundreds were fined and imprisoned before Cromwell removed the pressure for prosecution. Perhaps the main effect of the law was to drive a great many ardent religious disputants out of England.

Already out of England, but nevertheless imposing grave threats from afar, was Cardinal Reginald Pole. He and Pope

Paul III missed no opportunity to bring trouble to King Henry, urging everything from a boycott of English trade to outright military invasion. It was believed that Cardinal Pole was still in contact with his relatives in England and was working deviously through them. The cardinal's youngest brother, Geoffrey Pole, was arrested and either tortured or threatened with torture. Finally, when given a promise that he would not be executed, he gave much damaging evidence against his relatives and a few friends. As a result, the cardinal's elder brother, Henry, Lord Montague; Henry Courtenay, the Marquess of Exeter; Sir Edward Neville; and a few commoners were arrested, charged with treason, tried, and executed. Also arrested and imprisoned was Lady Margaret Pole, the Countess of Salisbury, the mother of Cardinal Pole and his two brothers. The Earl of Southampton and the Bishop of Ely, who carried out the lady's arrest, reported: "We assure your lordship we have dealt with such a one as men have not dealt withal before us. We may call her rather a strong and constant man than a woman. For in all behavior howsoever we have used her, she has showed herself so earnest, vehement, and precise, that more could not be."

There was so little evidence against the Countess of Salisbury that Cromwell was very reluctant to try her. Many thoughtful people were profoundly shocked by his solution. Parliament would do whatever its masters demanded and without trial, without evidence, without confession, the members of Parliament passed a bill of attainder against the countess and a few other people against whom little evidence was available. As a result of this "conviction by vote," she was put into prison, where she languished for two years before she was beheaded.

While these events had been going on in England, Thomas Cromwell had been searching for a suitable bride for King Henry—one who would please the king personally and would also bring advantages in diplomacy. One of the first prospective brides was Mary of Guise, daughter of the French Duke of Guise and widow of the Duke de Longueville. She was young and attractive, but two major difficulties stood in the way of her marriage to King Henry. Being closely related to the royal family of France, she would have to have the approval of King Francis I to take part in so important a foreign marriage. Perhaps even more important was the fact that she was already engaged to King James V of Scotland, who was King Henry's nephew. King Francis hoped that the marriage of his young kinswoman to James V would lead to a permanent alliance between France and Scotland, so he lost no time in forbidding the engagement of King Henry VIII to Mary of Guise.

King Henry then proposed that a large reception be held at Calais, where he could serve as host and meet noble French-women. King Francis would not hear of it. To him, the sugges-tion was shocking—sending the best and noblest ladies of his kingdom across the border into English-owned territory, like goods submitted on approval to the English king. He sent his ambassador, the Sieur de Castillon, to suggest that King Henry send a trusted representative to meet and report on the various ladies involved.

King Henry objected. "By God," he exclaimed, "I trust no one but myself. This thing touches me too near. I wish to see them and to know them for some time before deciding."

It was now Castillon's turn to be shocked. "Perhaps, Sire," he said, "you would like to try them one after the other and keep the one you found to be the most agreeable. Is that not the way the Knights of the Round Table used to treat the ladies in this country in olden times?"

The idea of the reception was quietly dropped.

France was not the only country that might provide a bride. If King Henry could not locate a French lady attractive enough to please him and highborn enough to draw King Francis to his side and away from Emperor Charles V, perhaps there was someone in the empire who might draw the emperor away from Francis and thus serve to break up the alliance against England and substitute for it one which included England. The order went out to locate such a woman.

In the court of the Emperor Charles there lived a sixteen-year-old widow who seemed an excellent prospect. Christina was the daughter of the former King Christian II of Denmark, who had been deposed for favoring the common people of his country over the nobility. Christina had become a duchess at fourteen when Emperor Charles V, who was her uncle, compelled her to marry the elderly and dying Duke of Milan. Half a year later the duke died and gratefully left his duchy of Milan to the emperor, to be a new part of the Holy Roman Empire. Now the tall, attractive, widowed Duchess of Milan was available for another marriage.

King Henry had never met the Duchess of Milan but what he had heard about the lady interested him greatly. Still, he did not want her, sight unseen. There was, in his court, a famous German portrait painter, Hans Holbein the Younger, who had come from Basel in 1526 to escape a severe financial depression and a series of religious persecutions. Holbein could paint her portrait. Today, a Holbein portrait is worth thousands of dollars, but King Henry paid the artist a mere thirty pounds a year to paint whatever pictures the king desired. Holbein was sent to Brussels, and in time he returned with a lovely portrait of the tall and comely duchess. King Henry was so pleased that he promptly had the picture hung on his bedroom wall.

When one of King Henry's representatives brought the duchess an offer of marriage from the king, she was well aware of the fates of his three previous queens, and she wanted no part of any such tragedy. Said she, "If I had a head to spare, I might accept him." She would scarcely have been so flip had Emperor

Charles been actively urging her to become King Henry's bride. The emperor was doing no such thing. Milan was a sensitive and troublesome part of his empire, and he did not want King Henry to have an excuse for meddling there. He also harbored a genuine suspicion that such a marriage might not be legal, since Christina was his niece and King Henry's first wife, Catherine of Aragon, had been his aunt. The two ladies were too closely related for comfort. Both he and his niece, Christina, were aware of the then widely circulated rumor that Queen Catherine of Aragon had been quietly murdered. It was this which led the duchess to exclaim, "My Council suspecteth that my great-aunt was poisoned, that the second was innocently put to death, and the third lost for lack of keeping in her childbed." It is not surprising that the lady and her uncle were anxious to delay or to avoid Christina's marriage to King Henry VIII.

King Henry read the situation aright. Said he, "The Emperor is knitting one delay to the tail of another."

In June 1538, the delays became outright cancellation when it was learned that King Francis I and Emperor Charles V had signed a ten-year truce and were listening to the urgings of Pope Paul III and Cardinal Reginald Pole, who wanted crusades launched against the various Protestant powers, including England.

There were other possibilities on the continent of Europe. A year earlier, in 1537, John Hutton, the English envoy at Brussels, sent a report to Thomas Cromwell, saying, "The Duke of Cleves hath a daughter, but I hear no great praise either of her personage nor beauty." But Thomas Cromwell was encouraged. To him, her lack of beauty and unwinning personality were trivial details. Of far greater importance was the situation in Cleves and the surrounding lands about the mouth of the Rhine. Since Hutton's report, the Duke of Cleves had died, leaving his title and his duchy to his young son, William, the brother of the lady whom Hutton had mentioned. From a religious point of view, Duke William of Cleves was in much the same situation as King Henry, since he refused to subject himself to the Catholic leadership of the pope but also opposed the Protestant teachings of Martin Luther. Cleves and England would probably both be prime targets of any crusade launched and led by King Francis and Emperor Charles. Young Duke William was trying to do something about this by forming a league of German states along the lower Rhine. Thus far, there seemed little likelihood of the new league rivaling the Holy Roman Empire, for Duke William and his near neighbors lacked both money and military power, but his ambition was high and his aims were favorable to England. With their families united by marriage, could not King Henry and Duke William create a third power in Europe capable of checking the dreaded alliance of France and the empire?

Inspired by his great dream of alliance, Cromwell did not hesitate to give King Henry a glowing report about the lady from Cleves. In place of Hutton's comments, he assured his king that, "Every man praiseth the beauty of the same lady, as well for the face as for the whole body, above all other ladies excellent. One amongst others . . . said that she excelleth as far the duchess [Christina, Duchess of Milan] as the golden sun excelleth the silvery moon." He then went on to explain the advantages to Henry and to England. He even gave a glowing description of the duke's eleventh century castle of Schwanenburg (Swan's Castle), dwelling upon its great importance and the part it had played in the ancient legend of Lohengrin and completely omitting the important facts that the castle was now an almost-uninhabitable ruin and that the duke, its owner, was virtually bankrupt.

King Henry was intrigued but cautious. He sent Holbein to Cleves to paint a portrait of the Lady Anne. Arriving at Schwanenburg, the artist found that the duke had not one unmarried sister but two, Anne and Amelia. Wishing to serve his king well, he painted portraits of both of them, but being an artist and wishing to serve art well he made both of them as attractive as the subject matter permitted. Henry studied both pictures carefully, selected Anne as his choice, and had her portrait hung in his bedroom in place of the picture of the Duchess of Milan.

Things now moved quickly, for King Henry had been for two years without a queen, and he was anxious to substitute a living wife for the painted figures which hung on his bedroom wall. The marriage treaty was signed on October 6, 1539, after Henry had been informed of his prospective brother-in-law's poverty and had agreed to forgo any dowry. Early in December, Anne arrived at Calais, but the December weather made the Channel so rough that the bride-to-be stayed for two weeks. On December 27, the weather changed, and she traveled to Rochester.

Henry, eager to meet his bride, went to Rochester to meet her. He went in disguise, for it was not yet the proper time for the bride and groom to meet. With him he brought eight of his courtiers, also disguised, and magnificent sable furs as New Year's gifts.

The first glance of his prospective bride horrified King Henry, who was immediately struck by her resemblance to one of the great dray horses which his people were accustomed to import from Flanders, in the same Lower Rhine region as Cleves. To him, from this point on, she was "the great Flemish mare," though there is no evidence that he ever used the term in her presence. He tried to speak to her but found that her only language was German, which he could not speak. After a very few minutes of growing disappointment, he fled, still clutching the furs he had brought her. The next day, they were delivered to her with a coldly polite note of welcome.

In spite of the king's very evident disappointment, Anne continued on toward Greenwich, where she was to marry Henry the very next day.

Anne of Cleves, Henry's fourth wife. (Portrait by Hans Holbein the Younger)

King Henry, meanwhile, was frantically searching for some excuse to call off the wedding. To aid in this attempt, the wedding date was set back two days, to January 6. The only possibility seemed to lie in the fact that she had earlier been promised to the son of the Duke of Lorraine, and therefore might not be free to marry another man. This hope disappeared when it was revealed that the "promise" had been made when the proposed bride was two and her groom-to-be three, that nothing more had been done about it since, and that Lorraine's son was now married to someone else and had a family of his own.

King Henry berated everyone who had had anything to do with the situation, including even the naval officer who had been in charge of bringing Anne across the Channel. To Cromwell, he exclaimed: "I have been ill-handled. . . . If it were not that she is come so far into my realm, and the great preparations that my state and people have made for her, and for fear of making a ruffle in the world, and of driving her brother into the hands of the Emperor and the French King, I would not now marry her."

The wedding took place on January 6, 1540. In spite of King Henry's lack of enthusiasm, it was magnificently staged. Five thousand uniformed horsemen rode in the procession, and guests and participants were beautifully and picturesquely dressed. The king played his part well, clasping her tenderly after Archbishop Cranmer had proclaimed them man and wife, kissing her, and addressing her as "sweetheart." There was, however, more diplomacy than genuine affection in his gestures.

The married life of King Henry and the new Queen Anne was strange. She did her best to make it a success but it was to no avail. Though they slept together on many nights, and though Henry desperately wanted and needed heirs, he was repelled by her homeliness. As for Queen Anne, she was quite content to have it so, for she had had no experience with men and felt timid in the presence of her husband.

Unfortunate as the marriage was, it was worse for King Henry than for Queen Anne. It was Henry who was accustomed to love and was desperately anxious for an heir. The passage of time was working strongly against him. Queen Anne, for all her difficulties, was far happier in England than she had been in Cleves.

Someone had to be punished for arranging this unhappy affair, and Thomas Cromwell was the person made to suffer. His punishment, though, had to wait until there was an excuse that did not cast an unfavorable light on the king. When rumors spread abroad that the common-born minister was in trouble, King Henry squelched them by making Cromwell a nobleman, with the title Earl of Essex.

The foreign tension lessened. Emperor Charles V came to the end of his long and worrisome visit to the court of King Francis I and went home. It was now possible to punish Thomas Cromwell and to get rid of Queen Anne without creating too much of a "ruffle in the world." Besides having arranged the marriage to the German princess, Cromwell had handled his powers in a fast, loose manner and, in addition, had taken for himself a goodly share of the treasures supposedly seized for his master, the king. This could well be considered treason.

Cromwell himself devised the means of bringing about his own destruction. The bill of attainder required no trial, no jury, no presentation of evidence. It had worked against Margaret, Countess of Salisbury, and it would work just as well against its own author.

King Henry moved fast. A few trusted intimates were taken into confidence and given specific tasks to perform. Thomas Howard, Duke of Norfolk—who had always detested Cromwell —was one of them. Bishop Gardiner was another. To Sir Thomas

Wriothesley (Risley) was given the task of forging letters which could be used to prove that Cromwell was laying plans to supersede England's religion with extreme Lutheranism, imported from the Rhineland area. So discreet were the plotters that Cromwell received no hint of what was afoot, though his highly developed instincts led him to sense danger.

Thomas Cromwell had staked everything on the success of the marriage to the princess from Cleves and the formation of the Lower Rhine alliance and had lost. That he knew, for it was now clear that a real marriage would never exist between King Henry and Queen Anne. What Cromwell did not know was that this state of affairs would soon come to an end. Already, the king was interested in a certain young lady of the court. Catherine Howard, thirty years younger than Henry, had met him and captivated him at a private party held for that very purpose at the home of Bishop Gardiner. Now, it became important to the King to be rid of the woman who stood between him and Catherine Howard. This was a situation which boded no good for the man who had maneuvered him into his situation of bondage, especially when one considers the fact that Catherine Howard's uncle, who was adroitly pushing her toward a crown, was none other than Cromwell's bitter enemy, Thomas Howard, Duke of Norfolk.

On the morning of June 10, 1540, Cromwell and other members of the Privy Council were walking toward Westminster to attend a meeting of Parliament when a sudden gust of wind blew his hat from his head. By custom, the others in the group should have removed their hats, but none did; all but he were aware of what was about to happen. Picking up his hat, he glared about him, his lip curling with disdain. "A high wind, indeed, to blow my bonnet off and keep all yours on!"

They went on in silence. At dinner, none of the men at Cromwell's table spoke to him—a fact which must have made him uneasy, though he said nothing. Outside the dining hall, people were waiting for him with requests and petitions, so he stopped to hear them while the others went on ahead to the meeting. It was well over an hour before he was free to join them. He found them hard at work, not having awaited his arrival. As he took his seat, he angrily exclaimed, "You were in a great hurry, gentlemen, to begin."

The Duke of Norfolk spun around. "Cromwell," he shouted, "do not sit there! Traitors do not sit with gentlemen!"

The word "traitors" was a signal. As Cromwell gazed in amazement at the duke, six soldiers and an officer entered the chamber and advanced upon him, while the Dukes of Norfolk and Southampton seized him. As the soldiers reached his side, he ceased his resistance and looked frantically from face to face. "So this is the reward of my services!" he exclaimed, bitterly. "So I am a traitor! On your consciences, *am* I a traitor? I have never thought to offend His Majesty, but since this is my treatment, I renounce all pardon. I only ask the King not to make me languish long."

There was no sympathy in the group surrounding him. Feeling certain that he was doomed, he permitted himself to be escorted through a "water door" of Westminster to a boat, in which he was rowed down the Thames to London Tower.

As Cromwell saw it, his one chance lay in cooperating fully and effectively with the king. Consequently, he uttered no protest and no reproaches when word reached him that King Henry had seized his lands, his houses, his wealth, and all his personal possessions for his own personal use. A further opportunity came when the king asked his aid in working out grounds for divorce from Anne of Cleves. True, there had been a hint that if he cooperated in this final assignment he would die quickly and painlessly under the axe and that if he did not he would have the worst of deaths, being hanged, drawn, and quartered. Nevertheless, he went beyond the mere routine which would have spared him this and prepared a magnificent thoughtful analysis and masterful presentation. Only at the very end did he include anything in his own behalf: "Written at the Tower, this Wednesday, the last of June, with the heavy heart and trembling hand of Your Highness's most heavy and most miserable prisoner and poor slave, Thomas Cromwell. Most gracious prince, I cry for mercy, mercy, mercy."

No mercy was forthcoming. King Henry used the presentation and disregarded the appeal. On July 28, Cromwell was taken to Tyburn for execution. As he said his few, last prayers—using, be it noted, the Catholic forms—he saw his friend, the poet Thomas Wyatt, weeping among the spectators. At this point, Cromwell uttered what was probably the greatest truth of his life: "Oh, Wyatt, do not weep, for if I were not more guilty than thou wert, when they took thee, I should not be in this pass."

The axe was swung. One wonders whether this brought satisfaction to a lady still awaiting execution, Lady Margaret Pole, Countess of Salisbury, for whose conviction Cromwell had conceived the very form of legal maneuver which had subsequently been used against him.

The moves to rid King Henry of his unwanted queen had gone rapidly ahead. Not long after Cromwell's arrest, the Dukes of Suffolk and Southampton and Sir Thomas Wriothesley paid a visit to Queen Anne. When the queen saw who her visitors were she feared that she, too, was to be arrested and executed. With a cry of terror, she fainted. When she was restored to consciousness, she learned that her fears were groundless. Though King Henry did wish to be rid of her as a wife, she would be treated with the greatest consideration. When would she like to return to Cleves? Recovering her self-possession, she declared that she would not. England was a better place to live and she would stay. Eventually, a most agreeable solution was found. Queen Anne accepted the divorce that had been worked out with Cromwell's aid and accepted the new title of Madame de Cleves in place of queen. She was now to be regarded as the king's sister and honored more highly than any woman in the kingdom, save the current queen and Henry's daughters. Two magnificent manor houses, Blechingley and Richmond, were assigned to her, with all furnishings and servants, and she was granted an annual income of four thousand pounds. A small fortune of jewels and clothing was added, and she was an embarrassingly happy woman.

# 11
# A ROSE WITHOUT A THORN

I
N accordance with his usual custom, King Henry VIII found something pleasant and diverting to do while Thomas Cromwell was being beheaded. On that day, July 28, 1540, the king was quietly being married at Oatlands Castle, some distance from London.

Henry's new bride was Catherine Howard, whom he fatuously described as "a blushing rose without a thorn." With ironic self-confidence, he had also coined for her a motto: *Non autre volonté que la sienne* (no other will but his).

The royal couple were almost spectacularly mismatched. King Henry was forty-nine years old, huge from overeating and over-drinking; limping about on his ulcerated leg, often with the aid of a staff; bearded, puffy; cynical and completely amoral, believing that whatever he wished to do was right and whatever he disapproved was evil; founder of a church that was neither Catholic nor Protestant and denied the leadership of anyone but himself. As the German Protestant leader Martin Luther put it, "Squire Harry wishes to be God and do whatever he pleases."

Standing beside her husband, Henry's fifth bride appeared even tinier than she was. Barely nineteen years of age, she had the clear, unspoiled complexion of youth; dark eyes; full, sensual lips, always smiling or ready to smile; and a mass of soft, auburn hair. Like all of the Howards, she tended to favor the Catholic aspects of her country's religion rather than the Protestant. She was in love with being a queen, with receiving valuable gifts and vast properties, with having a king in love with her, and with all of the head-turning deference and consideration that were now her due. King Henry, of course, felt that she was in love with him and him alone.

There was no question, though, that King Henry was in love with Catherine. His youth seemed to be renewed, and he took the greatest joy in plying her with gifts and in indulging her every whim. As Charles de Marillac, the French ambassador, reported to those at home in Paris, "The King is so amorous of Catherine Howard that he cannot treat her well enough and caresses her more than he did the others."

Even with his new bride, though, King Henry did not forget affairs of state. The prisons were overcrowded; many people were locked up for religious statements or practices. To make way for other prisoners, the king decreed that six of these should be executed on July 30, the second day after his wedding. To demonstrate the impartiality of his government, three of the six had to be Catholics and three, Protestants. The executions were open to the public. Accordingly, six prisoners were duly selected and were drawn from London to nearby Tyburn on hurdles. Once there, before the eyes of a large assembled group, the three Protestants were all fastened to a single, upright stake and burned alive. The three Catholics were hung, drawn, and quartered. King Henry and Catherine were not present.

Technically, Catherine Howard was not yet queen, even though she was the legal wife of King Henry. Because of the quiet and almost surreptitious nature of their wedding, she had not yet gone through the ceremony of being crowned. Summer would be a bad time to do it, because of the presence of the plague in and around London, but the king planned to hold his bride's coronation at the earliest practical moment, perhaps in the fall. Meanwhile, there was no reason why she should not receive all the rights and honors due a fully crowned queen, which she soon would be.

Catherine Howard had an open, generous nature, and she wished to be friends with everyone. Her approaches to Princess Mary, though, were not well received. Mary had maintained reasonably good relations with Queen Jane Seymour and Queen Anne of Cleves, but she refused to extend any courtesies to this new wife of her father, who was so much younger than she. The princess was not well, and she was extremely depressed over the latest developments in the long-continued search for a proper husband for her. The two most recent candidates, to whom she was being offered without any personal say in the matter, were Emperor Charles V and Charles, Duke of Orleans, the third son of King Francis I. Both, to her distress, had shown strong disapproval of her "illegitimacy," a purely artificial by-product of King Henry's contrived divorce from Queen Catherine of Aragon. It is not surprising, therefore, that Princess Mary was in no mood to undertake a new and joyous friendship with the woman who was currently taking her late and lamented mother's place in the kingdom.

Precisely the opposite was Catherine's reception by Anne of Cleves, who had so recently been Queen Anne of England. The two liked each other from the start. In late December, on the first anniversary of her original meeting with King Henry, Anne rode over from her manor house at Richmond with two richly caparisoned horses for King Henry. Catherine insisted that she stay to supper, so the three sat down together to an informal meal after Henry had greeted his recent wife with a "brotherly" kiss. Everything went pleasantly. Later, when the king had gone to bed, musicians were summoned and Catherine and Anne danced hand in hand, for hours. It was the beginning of a genuine friendship.

Other women, not previously seen at court, presently appeared and became ladies-in-waiting to Catherine Howard. Several of these were her girlhood friends who, like her, had been sent to live at Horsham House, in the care of her elderly relative, the Dowager Duchess of Norfolk, and had later had what amounted to a postgraduate course in courtly living at Lambeth Palace. These young women, as a group, shared many memories and more than a few secrets.

In the days when Thomas Cromwell had been in power, ardent Protestantism had flourished in England. It had been fashionable to suppress "papist practices," and such suppression had met with government approval. Now, with the fall and execution of the once-powerful minister, there was a strong reaction against such activities and even against pointed criticism of Catholicism. The king's new wife was from the strongly Catholic Howard family, and Henry was now swinging, pendulumlike, in that direction.

By way of demonstrating his evenhandedness in religious matters, the king now set about arresting those who had been expressing their anti-Catholicism too strongly. Among those seized were a number of prominent citizens who had received important appointments under Cromwell: Sir Thomas Wyatt, the ambassador to Spain; Sir John Wallop, the ambassador to France; Sir Ralph Sadler, the ambassador to Scotland; and others of like or lesser rank. These men went to the Tower with bound wrists, like common criminals, while the mob, urged on by Bishop Bonner of London, shouted for their deaths.

Sir Thomas Wyatt was the natural spokesman for the group. He was not only a prominent statesman but also a world-renowned poet, who had introduced the sonnet form into English literature. Without hesitation, this master of language unleashed his tongue and pen in his own defense and that of his associates, sparing the feelings of no one, even the king, in his denunciation of the injustice being committed. To most people, it must have looked as though all he would accomplish would be some worse form of torture in the deaths that he and his friends would meet.

Sir Thomas Wyatt's protests touched the heart of Catherine Howard. He was an old and admired friend, who had written beautiful verse to her cousin Anne Boleyn and had narrowly escaped fatal implication in Anne's downfall and death. Although he was charged with attacking her own religion, she bravely if not foolishly undertook to intercede for him and for his friend Wallop. She had earlier risked her husband's wrath by sending articles of clothing and comfort to the condemned Countess of Salisbury, awaiting execution in the Tower. Now she took an even greater risk by defending this man who, not once but twice, had performed the usually fatal act of arousing the king's ire.

It was a very good thing for Wyatt, for Wallop, and for Catherine herself that King Henry VIII was still so deeply and fondly in love with his bride that he found it nearly impossible to deny her anything. It was also a good thing for the endangered three that certain Catholics in the northern part of the country chose this time to criticize the English government and to perform lawless acts against it. Henry felt, at the same time, indulgent toward Catherine, somewhat sympathetic with the enemies of the troublemaking faction in the north, and secure enough to be able to afford a little "weakness"—his term for mercy. Accordingly, he forgave both Wyatt and Wallop, though on the condition that both confess their "guilt" and that Wyatt take back his discarded wife, whose sister was a close and admired friend of Henry's. The conditions were gratefully accepted, and the men went free.

The Catholic disturbances in the north; the growing influence of the aggressive, Catholic Howard family; and the overreaction of Catholics throughout the country following Cromwell's downfall and death gave King Henry some second thoughts about the execution of his energetic minister. He missed Thomas Cromwell. It had been convenient and reassuring to have so strong a hand upon the helm. As he remembered it, he personally had had nothing to do with this unfortunate occurrence. Others had engineered it and had misled him into giving his assent. Wailed the king: "On light pretexts, by false accusations, they made me put to death the most faithful servant I ever had."

There were, however, no regrets and no second thoughts about the seizing of Cromwell's vast estate. Some of the lands and other valuables that had been taken were included in the great abundance being lavished on Catherine Howard. The rest remained in Henry's personal possession. Whether or not Thomas Cromwell had been falsely accused, the Cromwell family would see no part of the confiscated estate.

Early in 1541, while winter still lingered on the English countryside, King Henry and his advisors decided that with the coming of warm weather the King and a large train of followers should visit the troublesome northern part of his country. Five years before, during the negotiations which brought the bloody Pilgrimage of Grace to an end, he had promised to visit that section and to remedy its wrongs, but he had not done so. The secondary purpose of the journey was to fulfill this promise. The primary purpose was to confer with King James V of Scotland, his nephew, and work out some advantageous arrangement with the Scottish government. As a by-product, the people of the troublesome northern shires would be impressed and intimidated by the great military force which would accompany the king. As a result, they would doubtless behave much better in the future.

The Great Northern Progress, as it was called, was supposed to begin early in June, but a late-departing winter delayed it week after week. During the enforced delay, King Henry grew steadily testier and harder to live with. Even Catherine Howard was not spared the lash of his tongue, hearing frequently the bitter complaint that she had not yet conceived the heir to the throne which he so desperately wanted. Adding to his sharp temper were his disappointment at the delay in his journey and the steady aggravation from the pain in his ulcerous leg.

Catherine, for her part, became desperately bored. The usual joys and pastimes of court life—the music, the dancing, the feasting, and the flirting—were missing, largely because of the king's evil mood and the emphasis placed upon the endless preparation for the Progress.

Into this potentially dangerous situation, Lady Rochford inserted herself. She was a lady-in-waiting who seemed to thrive on risky and unwholesome activities. Whenever there was court intrigue, she was seldom very far away. Her own husband—Anne Boleyn's brother—had met his death as a result of testimony which she had given at the late queen's trial. Now she sought to lessen her mistress's boredom by encouraging a flirtation between Catherine and handsome young Thomas Culpeper, one of the king's favorite attendants. On many an occasion, she stood watch while the two were together, guarding against a surprise interruption. When the Great Northern Progress should finally start, it seemed likely that the situation would continue, for both Lady Rochford and Thomas Culpeper were among the royal attendants who had been selected to go along.

At last the weather cleared and warmed, and the preparations for departure came to an end. Now only one thing remained to be done—a demonstration of King Henry's power over subjects who had displeased him. He wanted to have a salutary effect on any citizens of the northern shires who might object to his policies and activities. There were, in the Tower, a number of people who had long been held, awaiting just this sort of occasion. Prominent among them were Viscount Leonard Grey, former Lord Deputy of Ireland, who had dared to oppose some of the king's policies concerning the Irish; Lord Thomas Dacre, who had been a hero in the defeat of the Scots at Flodden Field but had later aroused Henry's ire by making an unauthorized truce with some of the rebels during the Pilgrimage of Grace; and Margaret, the Countess of Salisbury, whose crime was having mothered the Pole brothers. Viscount Grey and the Countess of Salisbury were condemned to be beheaded, as befitted members of the nobility. Lord Dacre was to be hanged as a common criminal. The case against him was weak, so an added charge was made that he had murdered a gamekeeper. In a meeting of the Council, the comment was made that "his property will be very profitable to the King."

The execution of Lady Margaret Pole, Countess of Salisbury, proved how very right the Earl of Southampton and the Bishop of Ely had been, two years before, in their report on her arrest. Her actions as she was being taken to the block were, indeed, far more like those of "a strong and constant man than a woman. . . . So earnest, vehement, and precise, that more could not be." In fact, this frail-looking, gray-haired lady, now seventy-two, fought with more strength and desperation than any man who was executed during King Henry's reign. Unlike so many sweet, resigned, and weeping ladies, she absolutely refused to lay her head upon the block: "That death is for traitors, and I was never such!" As the jailers laid hands on her to force her down, she struggled, shouted, and fought with fists and feet. More than once, they thought that they had her firmly down, with head on block, only to have her wrench herself aside as the axe descended. Each time this happened, she was grievously wounded, but not yet dead and not yet submissive. By the time a fatal blow was landed, severing her head from her body, a number of strong men were thoroughly exhausted and well spattered by her blood.

With these preliminaries out of the way, the Great Northern

Progress belatedly set forth. It was an imposing procession, numbering nearly five thousand people: the King and Catherine; courtiers, male and female; court attendants; soldiers, including knights, infantrymen, and artillerymen with their cannons; cooks; servants; and others. As it moved slowly northward, to awe the inhabitants, King Henry found enjoyment in slaughtering game birds and animals in enormous numbers. Catherine did not accompany him on these hunting expeditions.

Back at the court, certain worried people were conferring on the problems that had arisen following the execution of Thomas Cromwell. Chief among these were three Protestant leaders, Archbishop Cranmer, Sir John Seymour, and Sir Thomas Seymour. Cranmer had been left in charge of the government during the king's absence. The Seymours were the brothers of Queen Jane Seymour and the uncles of her son, Prince Edward. They had long been confident that when King Henry VIII died they would be in a position to direct the running of the government through their nephew, who would then be King Edward VI. Now, though, the glorious dream was showing signs of fading out. The Protestant Seymours were no longer the favorites they once had been. King Henry had married Catholic Catherine Howard. She and her Howard relatives were now the favored ones. Worst of all, she was young and ardent, and there seemed every chance that she would have a healthy, robust son who would compete with frail, unhealthy Prince Edward for the throne.

Such was the worrying of the little group of three when a simple, earnest man named John Lassells came to see Archbishop Cranmer about a matter which was bothering his Puritan conscience. Lassells' sister Mary had formerly been employed as a nurse at Horsham House, under the old Duchess of Norfolk. When Lassells had suggested that his sister apply for a position under Queen Catherine Howard, Mary had exclaimed that she never would, "for the Queen is a light woman!" ("Light," in that sense, meant "immoral.") Pressed for details, Mary Lassells had then told her brother what, she said, everyone at Horsham House had known, that Catherine Howard had permitted her music master, Mr. Henry Manox, to caress her and to see a hidden mole in a place where no man, save a husband, should ever look. Later, a young man named Francis Dereham had come to her room on many nights and had climbed into bed with her. The duchess had known all this and had tried to punish her, but Catherine had laughed at the punishments and had continued her evil ways. Mary Lassells had not wanted to say anything about these things, but John had insisted, for he could never sleep with such guilt on his conscience, unrevealed to someone in authority.

Archbishop Cranmer passed on the shocking news he had received to the Seymours and to two members of the king's Council who had not accompanied Henry on the Progress. The Council members talked it over and agreed that the king must be told as soon as he reached home. They also very conveniently decided that a prominent churchman was just the person to inform the king. Much to his distress, Archbishop Cranmer was given the dangerous and unpleasant assignment.

At the same time, King Henry was undergoing a disappointment that was certain not to improve his disposition. He had invited his nephew King James V of Scotland to cross the border and meet him at York. All was in readiness there for another, though slightly smaller, Field of the Cloth of Gold. King James did not appear. Not unreasonably, he did not trust his uncle enough to venture across the border and into Henry's power, especially in view of the fact that he himself had no living descendants to succeed him on the throne of Scotland if he should be detained and unable to return home. It had taken King Henry seventy-eight days to travel from London to York. He waited another week, in growing irritation, then had his tented city disassembled and started south, toward home.

The homeward part of the Great Progress was accomplished much more rapidly than the journey north. The weather was growing cold, and there was much less incentive for side journeys and hunting sessions. By the end of October—less than six weeks —King Henry and his entourage arrived at Hampton Court. Despite his disappointments, the king was happy, suspecting nothing of the upsetting news awaiting him.

Archbishop Cranmer was by no means a bold and forthright person. He had no desire to appear before the king and tell him what had occurred. Instead, he wrote out the whole distressing story in full and thrust it into the king's hand as he was leaving Mass on All Souls' Day, November 2. In a few whispered words, he requested Henry not to unfold the paper until he was alone in his room.

The expected explosion did not occur. King Henry simply could not believe the dreadful things written in that paper about his little "rose without a thorn." Some scandalmonger must be trying to spread false and malicious reports about his wife! He sent for Cranmer, hoping to learn who the character assassin was. The archbishop, trembling and unhappy, repeated the story as he had written it. The king could see that Cranmer believed it to be true, and for the first time he became worried. If the story was true, and Catherine had been involved with Manox and Dereham, then she was guilty of having concealed her unchaste girlhood from the king.

King Henry took a few of his most trusted councillors into his confidence: Sir Thomas Wriothesley, Anthony Browne, Lord Thomas Audley, the Dukes of Norfolk and Sussex, the Earl of Southampton, Bishop Gardiner, and, of course, Archbishop Cranmer. A quiet investigation was launched. Witnesses were interviewed and, in some cases, mercilessly grilled. Dereham, who had fled from the country and had become a pirate in Ireland when he first learned that the king was going to marry Catherine Howard, had since found the courage to return and become her private secretary. He was arrested on a charge of piracy. Manox, the amorous music master, was also arrested and confined. Both men confessed to the deeds with which they were charged. Manox revealed that his dalliance had been brief, for he had been caught by the old duchess and had been summarily dismissed, without further opportunity to see Catherine. Dereham admitted that he had dallied long and frequently, coming to her bed at night, at first fully clothed but, on later occasions, removing his clothes. He excused himself and her, however, by asserting that there had been a promise of marriage between them.

Catherine had been confined to her rooms, with only four ladies-in-waiting and two chamberers in attendance. She had been deprived of her jewels and all but the simplest of her clothing. Here, early in the investigation, she was visited by Thomas Howard, Duke of Norfolk, seeking her confession. The duke was in a savage mood, for he could see his favored position with the king disappearing. Two of his nieces, Anne Boleyn and Catherine Howard, had become wives of King Henry VIII, and both had disgraced themselves. The more he talked, the angrier he became. Catherine, appalled by her uncle's tirade, became hysterical and frantically denied everything.

After a suitable interval, Archbishop Cranmer came to see her. He had conferred with the king and had been instructed to emphasize the dreadful things that she had done and the peril of her present position. If she should cooperate, he was then empowered to hold out to her the hope that the king, her loving husband, would pardon her and would eventually restore her to favor. When the archbishop saw her overwrought state, though, he chose to alter the procedure. In the hope of calming her, he mentioned the possibility of pardon at the very beginning.

Taken by surprise, and reassured by Cranmer's unctuous voice, Catherine broke down completely, freely and tearfully confessing everything to which the two men had testified, with one exception: she would not admit that any understanding concerning a marriage had ever existed between Dereham and her. By doing this, she greatly increased Dereham's peril but lessened her own. The sin of being promiscuous as a young girl was far less serious than it would have been to accept the king's proposal of marriage without informing him that a marriage understanding already existed with another man. Such an admission would almost certainly have led to her being divorced and, quite possibly, sent to a nunnery for the rest of her life.

As Catherine confessed, Archbishop Cranmer quietly wrote down everything she said. Unguardedly, lulled by the churchman's apparent deep sympathy, she signed the statement in her childish scrawl. Not until he was gone, bearing the incriminating paper with him, did she begin to realize what she had done. Panic-stricken, she sent him another note stating that everything Dereham had done to her had been done by force, without her consent.

Not until those who had examined the witnesses and the accused gathered with King Henry to sum up the evidence and dovetail the various accounts was the king completely sure that the woman he loved so deeply was guilty. The hidden mole on Catherine's body was the thing which finally convinced him. Manox had described exactly where it was situated. Henry knew that mole and knew from the description that Manox did, too.

Thus far, consideration had been given only to Catherine's misdeeds with Manox and Dereham, in the years before her marriage. No one had openly raised any question about possible adulterous activities since she had been King Henry's wife. Some minds, though, were busily at work. An informative message sent by the Council members to Baron William Paget,

English representative in Paris, ended with these ominous words: "Now you may see what was done before marriage. God knoweth what has been done since."

As usually happens in such a case, one accusation led to another. A new name was introduced into the case during the questioning of Marget Morton, one of Catherine's chamberers. Said she: "I never mistrusted the Queen until, at Hatfield, I saw her look out of her chamber window on Master Culpeper after such sort that I thought there was love between them."

This was innocent enough—a glance not even returned, perhaps not even realized by the recipient. At about the same time, though, something far more damnatory was added. During the continued questioning of Francis Dereham, he was asked if he had continued to lie with the queen after her marriage, while he was serving as her private secretary. He said that he had not. When asked why he had not, he said it was because the queen was no longer in love with him but with Thomas Culpeper.

Culpeper had no warning at all. His first intimation that his name had come into the case came when he felt the strong hands of King Henry's constables closing on his arms. Catherine would gladly have warned him, but she had had no opportunity to do so.

At their trials, both Dereham and Culpeper steadfastly denied that they had had any carnal contact with Catherine after her marriage to the king. Even when tortured on the rack—a completely illegal procedure—they continued to protest their innocence. Nor could any witness testify that he or she had witnessed such an act, though Lady Rochford, while denying that she had voluntarily aided in the secret "backstairs meetings," did offer the opinion that there must have been such relations between Catherine and Culpeper, judging by what she had seen.

At last Culpeper, badgered by the court and seeing no hope, issued a statement: "Gentlemen, do not seek to know more than that the King deprived me of the thing I love best in the world, and, though you may hang me for it, she loves me as well as I love her, though up to this hour no wrong has ever passed between us. Before the King married her, I thought to make her my wife, and when I saw her lost to me, I was like to die, as you all know how ill I was. The Queen saw my sorrow and showed me favor, and when I saw it, tempted by the Devil, I dared one day while dancing to give her a letter, and received a reply from her in two days, telling me she would find a way to comply with my wish. I know nothing more, my lords, on my honor as a gentleman."

At the word "gentleman," the Duke of Norfolk sneered aloud —a part of the campaign he had been carrying on ever since the first evidence concerning his niece had been unearthed. He, Thomas Howard, wanted to be completely dissociated from his erring niece, and he did not hesitate to say repeatedly that she should suffer death by burning.

Moving as Culpeper's statement was, it bore the seeds of death for Catherine and for him. While denying the evildoing with which they were charged, it openly admitted both his and her intention to commit adultery, and in this case the intent was almost equivalent to the deed itself.

The court found both Dereham and Culpeper guilty and sentenced them to the ultimate in frightful deaths—to be hanged, drawn, and quartered.

The revelation that Catherine had intended to commit adultery with Culpeper seemed to release furies within the soul of King Henry. At one point, he called for a sword with which to kill her personally. At another, he exclaimed, "That wicked woman! She never had such delight in her lovers as she shall have torture in her death!" He did not mean either threat. What he actually felt was not so much hate as grief. He had loved Catherine Howard and had lavished gifts and affection upon her. Even so, she had turned against him. It was a blow from which he would never completely recover.

Nor did he feel hate for Tom Culpeper, who had long been his favorite personal attendant. When his fury had subsided, he modified the young man's sentence. Under the circumstances, he had to die, but the frightful fate that had been decreed was changed to the quicker and kinder method of beheading with an axe. The king refused, though, to modify Dereham's sentence, saying that he deserved no such mercy. This man had not been one of his favorites.

Catherine was now moved from Hampton Court to Syon House, a former nunnery of the Brigittine Order located near Richmond Palace. There she was confined in greatly reduced but not uncomfortable circumstances. Lady Rochford was also confined there, both as a prisoner and as a spy. She had been instructed to send reports to the king of every important thing that Catherine said. Her cooperation in this had been obtained through hints that if she revealed something of importance things might go better with her. In view of the lady's evidence in the trial, one wonders how the two prisoners got along during their two months at Syon House.

King Henry had learned a great deal since the execution of Anne Boleyn six years before. Then, he had lost much popularity and had been roundly criticized for putting his wife to death. This time, he left the unwanted initiative to his councillors and to Parliament, while he went on a journey to parts unknown, accompanied only by a small group of musicians and a few close personal attendants. When condemnation was made, he would not even be present.

Catherine Howard received no trial. Parliament reconvened in January 1542 and passed one of those convenient bills of attainder that had been so ingeniously applied by Cromwell to achieve the death of unwanted persons and by others to achieve

his death. This bill, though, was a widely sweeping one. It condemned Catherine Howard and Lady Rochford to death by beheading for committing and abetting treason against the king,
the Dowager Duchess of Norfolk for having concealed Catherine's activities at Horsham House, and assorted other members
of the Norfolk clan for various real or imaginary actions in
connection with Catherine's treason. Except for Catherine and
Lady Rochford, the attainted Norfolks were to lose all of their
property, which would go to the king, and were to be imprisoned
for life. The property was duly seized and was retained, but the
imprisoned family members were eventually released. Only the
head of the family, Thomas Howard, Duke of Norfolk, was not
included in the bill. His early and violent condemnation of his
latest erring niece had been effective. He retained his office as
national treasurer, but his rise to power was checked at that
point and his ambitions remained unrealized.

Only very gradually did Catherine Howard come to realize the
full iniquity and foolishness of what she had done. When she
understood it, she became reconciled to her fate. Both houses
of Parliament had passed the bill of attainder providing for the
execution of the two women being held at Syon House. The
receipt of the news sent Lady Rochford into a screaming frenzy
which nearly unhinged her mind, but Catherine received it
calmly. Word came that the king was willing to grant her an
opportunity to appeal her case to Parliament, but she declined
to do it, saying that she had sinned and deserved to die. She
made only two requests: that her Howard relatives be not
blamed for her misdeeds and that "the execution shall be
secret and not under the eyes of the world." The first of these,
as we have seen, was not granted; the second was.

Catherine's mood of calm lasted during her remaining days
at Syon House. It ended when three barges appeared at the
water gate and Sir John Gage told her he had come to take her

Catherine Howard, Henry's fifth wife, on her way to the Tower of London. (Painting by E. F. Skinner)

and her companion to the Tower. Then there was brief rebellion, followed by weeping. Her distress continued in the Tower, causing a postponement of her execution from Friday, February 10, to Monday, the thirteenth. By Sunday afternoon, she was again composed. At her request, the block was brought to her room, and she was instructed on how she should place herself for the execution. She tried it several times, striving to be both correct and graceful.

The next morning, in the cold of a February sunrise, she went out to the courtyard where the execution would take place. Except for her uncle, the entire Council was there, and various other people as well, but no great throng, as she had feared. She made a brief speech: "Brothers, by the journey upon which I am bound, I have not wronged the King. But it is true that long before the King took me, I loved Culpeper, and I wish to God I had done as he wished me, for at the time the King wanted to take me, he urged me to say that I was pledged to him. If I had done as he advised me, I should not die this death, nor would he. I would rather have had him for a husband than be mistress of the world. But sin blinded me, and greed of grandeur, and since mine is the fault, mine also is the suffering, and my great sorrow is that Culpeper should have had to die through me."

She stopped, half-choked by her emotions, and turned to the headsman: "Pray hasten with thy office."

He knelt at her feet and asked her pardon for what he was about to do.

Still standing, Catherine added a few more words: "I die a queen, but I would rather die the wife of Culpeper. God have mercy on my soul. Good People, I beg you pray for me."

Suddenly, she fell to her knees and placed her head on the block. As her cousin Anne Boleyn had done six years before, she began to pray. The slashing axe cut her off in the midst of the first sentence.

Only after Catherine's body and head had been gathered up and borne away wrapped in black velvet was Lady Rochford brought to the courtyard. Her parting words were not without interest: "I am innocent of the crime of which I am accused, but I die justly because I lied long ago when I myself accused my husband George and the Queen Anne of incest."

Then she knelt, the axe came down, and her blood poured out to mix with that of Catherine Howard.

# 12
# THE AGING WARRIOR

THE pattern was familiar. To take his mind from the unpleasant subject of his wife's execution, King Henry kept himself busy planning a great reception to be held on the following Sunday. The day arrived, and the reception was held, the principal guests being twenty-six of the most beautiful noblewomen of the realm. The king served as the perfect host, and it was recorded that "he made them great and hearty cheer."

The "great and hearty cheer" must have contained a good deal of make-believe, for King Henry was not in a cheerful mood. He had been badly shaken by Catherine Howard's unfaithfulness—her preference for another man ahead of him. Now, he was older looking, more tired, and less well than before. His ulcerated leg impeded him more than he had ever permitted it to do. As for another wife, he had no plans for one and was strongly of the opinion that he would never want to marry again.

Nevertheless, Parliament—which had taken the onus of Catherine's condemnation from the kingly shoulders—also assumed the responsibility of making a repetition far less likely. Three laws were passed bearing directly on the subject. The first provided that any not previously married woman whom the king asked to be his wife would be guilty of high treason if she did not immediately inform His Majesty of any previous sexual experience.

The second provided that any person who was aware of such previous sexual experience on the part of a not previously married woman selected to be the king's bride, and who did not immediately report this fact to the authorities, should be guilty of high treason. The third provided that any Queen of England who should be unfaithful to her husband, or who should attempt to be, would be guilty of high treason. The penalty was the same for all three offenses. Whoever should be found guilty was to be taken to Tyburn and there hanged, drawn, and quartered unless His Majesty, in his infinite mercy, should graciously consent to substitute death by decapitation.

In view of the horrifying impact of these three laws on the womanhood of England, it was probably just as well that King Henry had no immediate plans for remarriage. The maiden ladies of the nobility were especially appalled. According to Lord Edward Herbert, of Cherbury, one of King Henry's earliest biographers, "They stood off as knowing in what a slippery estate they were, if the King, after receiving them to bed, should, through any mistake, declare them no maids."

But if King Henry was paying less attention than usual to the marriageable ladies of his and other realms, he was paying even closer attention to international affairs. This, too, was just as well. In Rome, Pope Paul III was doing his best to unite the great Catholic powers into a vast crusade—or, if necessary, a series of smaller crusades—to bring back into the fold those nations and parts of nations that had branched off and had accepted Protestant variations of Christianity. King Henry soon became well aware that he was a special target of the Pope's campaign. High up among the leaders of such a crusade would be Emperor Charles V of the Holy Roman Empire and King Francis I of France. Four years before, these two long-time rivals had signed a ten-year treaty of peace, and since that time they had been living in peace and apparent friendship. Either one, alone, was a powerful opponent. If both should come against England at once, things would be desperate indeed. To make matters worse, Scotland was an ally of France, so if war should come there would already be enemy forces on the island.

As King Henry watched the trend of affairs on the continent, he remained busy with affairs at home. There were many religious shadings within his kingdom, the two most important groups being those under Bishop Stephen Gardiner, who favored the Catholic teachings, and those under Archbishop Thomas Cranmer, who favored a moderate Protestantism and independence from the Pope and Rome. The king skillfully kept his central position between these extremes, balancing favors to one with favors to the other and suppression of one with suppression of the other. As a result, he retained at least nominal support from all groups. He also spent a good deal of time, energy, and money on strengthening the defenses of the kingdom, constructing forts to protect the leading seaports, and building up the fleet by the addition of new warships. Among these were a new *Great Harry*, to replace the topheavy experimental warship in which he had gone to the Field of the Cloth of Gold, and a new *Mary Rose* to replace the unfortunate first vessel of this name, sunk by the French *Cordelière* some thirty years before.

Meanwhile, the king's vigilance continued, and in time it brought results. The honeymoon between Charles V and Francis I began to show signs of coming to an end. The city of Algiers was a haven for Mediterranean pirates. Emperor Charles, stung by the loss of some of his ships, attacked the city and failed to take it. King Francis, encouraged by this sign of weakness, began to lay plans for an attack of his own, this one to be aimed at Milan, which had been under Charles's control for the past seven years. When this attack should take place, the "ten-year peace" would be over. Francis, seeking allies, committed the unheard-of breach of Christian manners by sending emissaries to work out a treaty with the Mohammedan Turks. Charles, hearing of the attempt, sent assassins to intercept and kill the emissaries. When the expected French and Empire representatives appeared before Henry, each seeking his support against the other, he managed to make both of them believe that he would remain neutral, no matter what happened between them.

Actually, King Henry had not the slightest intention of remaining neutral in any war which should break out between the emperor and Francis I. In June of 1542, he sent the Bishop of Westminster to hold talks with Charles V and to arrange a secret alliance. A year was allowed for preparations. Then, in June of 1543, both King Henry and Emperor Charles were personally to lead their armed .forces in a surprise invasion of France. Both armies were to strike directly for Paris. When King Francis had been beaten, King Henry was to receive as his share of the spoils the lands along the Bay of Biscay, north of Spain, which had been the possession of the Plantagenet Kings of England from the mid-twelfth through the fourteenth century. Emperor Charles was to get Burgundy.

Henry's first order of business in the year of preparation was the chastisement of Scotland, so there would be no invasion of England from the north while he was busy invading France. For this attempt, he had certain geographical advantages. The richest lands of Scotland lay just north of the Scottish-English border, whereas the English lands just south of that border were among the poorest. Hence, English raids into Scotland could do far more material damage than comparable Scottish raids into England. In addition, the Scottish capital of Edinburgh was within forty miles of the border, whereas London was more than two hundred fifty miles away and thus completely out of reach of raiding Scottish armies.

Though King James V was the nominal ruler of Scotland, Catholic Cardinal David Beaton, the Lord Privy Seal, was the power behind the throne. It was Beaton who had advised King James not to go south to meet his Uncle Henry on English soil, and thus had spoiled King Henry's second Field of the Cloth of Gold at York. Henry felt, quite rightly, that the cardinal was the principal obstacle between him and the take-over of the troublesome little kingdom to the north.

King James V, strongly backed by Cardinal Beaton, reacted with horror to King Henry's suggestion that Scotland do as England had done and break the hold of the Catholic Church of Rome on his country. The answer was no. James was neither ready nor anxious for war, but neither was he willing to permit Henry to take over his country. When, therefore, an opportunity was offered for a peace conference south of the border, he happily sent a delegation, though he did not go himself. The fact that his two infant sons had recently died, leaving him without an heir to follow him on the throne, led him and the cardinal to reject any such foolhardy venture into King Henry's power.

The members of the Scottish delegation cheerfully agreed to any and all suggestions made by the English, but after they had returned home nothing at all was done to implement the agreements. Gradually, King Henry and his advisors realized that the Scottish maneuvers had served only to gain time for the carrying out of Scottish preparations for war.

When it became evident that the Scots were not going to do as their representatives had indicated, King Henry ordered his armies to advance north across the border. One small group, in too much of a hurry, was cut off by the Scots at Haddonrig in August 1542 and was defeated. Five hundred of its members were taken prisoner. The main army, under Thomas Howard, Duke of Norfolk, did better, though it lacked the supplies it should have had. Crossing the border, Norfolk burned and ravaged for six days, then returned to feed and rest his tired, hungry army.

The main effect of Norfolk's raid was to anger the Scots to the point of striking back. In November, a Scottish army which may have numbered twenty thousand men crossed the border to lay waste as much of England as they could. The Scots were doughty fighters, but they did not cooperate well, and they had little group discipline. At Solway Moss, they met an English cavalry detachment. At once, a false rumor spread through the Scottish ranks that the whole English army was upon them. Panic spread, and the army turned to flee, only to find itself cut off by an inlet swollen to impassability by the incoming tide. Though only about twenty Scots were killed, upwards of twelve hundred were captured, including Cardinal Beaton, who had come to pronounce the Pope's interdict against England and her government while standing on English soil. The cardinal was one of a group of Scottish leaders who presently found themselves confined in the Tower of London.

Word of the defeat at Solway Moss reached King James as he was leading a considerable Scottish force to strike "a second blow" at the English. When his nobles learned that there had been no first blow, most of them broke camp and took their men homeward. James, abandoned, was forced to flee. He took refuge in Falkland Palace, where he waited, heartsick and discouraged, for the falling of the next blow.

Two blows fell on King James in rapid succession. Word came that his Queen, Marie of Guise, had had the child which he and she had been expecting. Instead of a boy, to replace the recently dead Scottish princes, it was a girl, whom the Queen had named Mary. "The De'il take it!" cried James, knowing now that he would never have a male heir to his throne. "The De'il take it!" Sick with the disappointment, he retired to his bed. Three days later, he was dead "of grief, regret, and rage," leaving as his heir the four-day-old girl baby who was already beginning to experience the tragic misfortunes which would become associated with her title of Mary, Queen of Scots.

Had King Henry chosen to, he could have sent his armies into Scotland and taken over the country with very little trouble. Instead, he tried finesse. Now that King James V was dead, the government of Scotland had fallen into the hands of a new governor, James Hamilton, Earl of Arran, who was ruling in the name of the newborn infant, Queen Mary. As a young man, the earl had been something of a rebel, declaring himself a Protestant and an opponent of Cardinal Beaton. Handled right, such a man should make an ideal agent, within the Scottish government, for carrying out Henry's rapidly maturing plans for the northern country.

What King Henry had in mind was a marriage contract between his six-year-old son, Prince Edward, and tiny Queen Mary of Scotland. In preparation for this, Queen Mary should be sent at once to England to be cared for and properly educated along King Henry's line of thinking. At the same time, Scotland should be breaking its ties with the Roman Catholic Church and adopting the sort of Protestantism which Henry had introduced into England. With these things accomplished, England and Scotland could peacefully merge into a single country with a single religion and a single ruling family. With Wales already in the fold and Scotland coming in, Henry's descendants would no longer be merely Kings of England but Kings of Great Britain —rulers of the entire island!

Everything seemed to favor the smooth operation of King Henry's plan. The Earl of Arran appeared thoroughly agreeable and offered no opposition to the procedures which were outlined for him to follow. The prisoners taken at Solway Moss were just as cooperative. They would go back to Scotland and would urge the acceptance of the wonderful English plan. To help in weaning Scotland from its spiritual dependence on Rome, King Henry and Archbishop Cranmer prepared a complete manual, outlining step by step the procedures that had worked so well in England. These instructions, plus copies of the English forms of ritual, were collectively known as *The King's Book*.

The results were disappointing. The liberated Scotsmen seemed to display far less enthusiasm when they had returned to their native heath than they had shown when they were involuntary guests of King Henry. True, they did obtain agreement that little Queen Mary should become the bride of Prince Edward, but they regretfully announced that her education for the position would have to be postponed. Instead of going to England right away, she would wait until she was ten years old, *then* visit the land of her fiancé. As for converting Scotland from a Catholic to a Protestant land, that would take much time. People do not readily give up the beliefs in which they have been raised.

Though King Henry was disappointed, he remained hopeful. At least, Scotland was peaceful and seemed friendly. He felt it safe to turn his back on the northern border in order to concentrate on some other items that were now clamoring for attention.

King Henry's England was a perilous place for men of temperament and genius. We have already noted the grim situation into which Sir Thomas Wyatt, the brilliant poet, blundered by speaking freely. He and a few of his associates were saved only by the intercession of Catherine Howard. Wyatt continued to create his poetic gems for a few months after being saved, but in the summer of 1542 he was sent to Falmouth by the king to meet an ambassador representing Charles V and to accompany him to court. The weather was hot and the ride was long. Wyatt developed a fever and died.

At about the same time, death claimed another and even greater genius. Hans Holbein the Younger was one of the most skilled and talented portrait painters who ever lived. Although the artist was deeply involved in two important unfinished paintings, and although London was experiencing one of its periodic sieges of the plague, King Henry sent him there on assignment. The artist caught the disease and quickly died. Because he was not a member of the nobility, he was not accorded the dignity of a separate burial. His body was burned, and his ashes were mixed with those of a number of other plague victims and buried in a common grave.

Henry Howard, the Earl of Surrey, inherited two things from the late Sir Thomas Wyatt: his place as leading poet of the day and his son, Sir Thomas Wyatt, the younger, who became Surrey's follower and his companion in roistering adventures about the streets of London. In one of his poems, "A Satire Against the Citizens of London," Surrey wrote:

> *London! Hast thou accused me*
> *Of breach of laws? The root of strife!*
> *Within whose breach did burn to see,*
> *So fervent hot, thy dissolute life . . .*

Besides being an inspired poet, Surrey was a troublemaker, but King Henry liked him and forgave him much. There is an incident which seems worth relating because it shows something of the poet and his friends and a great deal more about the harsh laws of the time. Surrey and Sir Edmund Knyvett had been playing tennis on the royal courts at Greenwich. With Surrey was one of his servants, who was making himself useful in a variety of ways. Something the servant did angered Knyvett, who struck the man and drew blood, probably from the nose. A trial was held. Surrey, calling upon his mastery of the language, spoke in behalf of his man and managed to win the case. In view of the fact that the blow had been struck on the royal courts, and was therefore a disrespectful gesture toward the host, King Henry, the judges assigned three harsh penalties: Knyvett was to be imprisoned until King Henry should give the word for his release, was to lose all his lands and goods, and was to have his right hand amputated!

On the day when the amputation was to take place, all was

in readiness—knife in place on the joint and mallet poised to drive it through—when Knyvett suddenly asked for a brief stay so that he might send a message to the king. The stay was granted, and the message was sent. It besought the King to change the sentence to the amputation of the left hand, "for if my right hand be spared I may hereafter do much good service to Your Grace, as shall please you to appoint." King Henry was so delighted by the loyalty expressed in the message that he promptly canceled all three penalties, permitting Sir Edmund to go free and unpunished.

The eighteen months following the execution of Catherine Howard constituted a period of growing unhappiness for King Henry. He was a bored and lonesome man with three children who needed an understanding woman to mother them. Princess Mary was twenty-six, still unmarried, technically illegitimate, thin, nervous, bitter, "the most unhappy lady in Christendom," to use her own phrase. Elizabeth, also technically illegitimate, was somewhat happier, a vibrant, intellectually active ten-year-old, but she, too, needed mothering. Six-year-old Prince Edward, whose health was a constant worry to his father, was overwhelmed with guides and tutors, but he needed a mother most of all. Despite his earlier proclamation that he would never marry again, King Henry was coming to realize that he had better take another wife, and a good one this time. His children needed her, and so did he.

Catherine Parr, the woman whom Henry needed, appeared in court early in 1543. As she had already been married twice, she was in no danger of running afoul of two of the three stern laws which Parliament had passed concerning royal wives, and her own quiet, moral character provided an excellent defense against the third. Her first husband, Lord Borough, had died many years before, leaving her a widow at seventeen. Her second, Lord Latimer, had died very recently. She had come to the court in company with Sir Thomas Seymour, a man with more vices than morals who was anxious to marry her and obtain the rather considerable fortune which she had inherited from her first two husbands.

Sir Thomas Seymour had already proposed marriage to Catherine Parr, but she had put him off, attracted by his dashing personality but repelled by his reputation. It was then that King Henry saw her and lost no time in asking her to be his queen. The idea caught her completely unprepared and very nearly bowled her over in the most literal of senses. Memories of Henry's first five wives must have crossed her mind: two divorced, two put to death, one dead following childbirth. Certainly, she was not unmindful of Parliament's new and frightful law regarding royal wives. Whatever her thoughts, she gasped and stammered, "It were better to be your mistress than your wife."

King Henry did not want a mistress. He wanted a wife to be his companion and his nurse, to love and to care for his much-neglected children, to see to the running of his household, to give advice from a woman's point of view on the numerous questions, foreign, domestic, and religious, arising every day. Catherine Parr was just what he wanted—moral, intelligent, level-headed, and with religious feelings much like his own, embracing neither extreme Catholicism nor extreme Protestantism but a blend of the two that permitted both an appreciation and a criticism of each. This was a wife who would bring peace, not trouble, to his home.

King Henry repeated his urgings, and Catherine Parr said yes. They were married on July 12, 1543, in the small room of the palace known as "the Queen's closet." Said she: "I, Catherine, take thee, Henry, to my wedded husband, to have and to hold from this day forward, for better for worse, for richer for poorer, in sickness and in health, to be bonair and buxom in bed and at board, till death us do part."

So they were married, she for the third time, he for the sixth. At fifty-two, King Henry was an old man. At thirty-one, Catherine Parr was settled and mature. Sir Thomas Seymour was glad to take a diplomatic position in the Netherlands, confident that if he should just wait long enough he would yet have his intended bride.

One of the first results of the marriage was the reuniting of the royal family, which had never really been together for any length of time. Princess Mary was living in the palace with her father, but Princess Elizabeth was at Hatfield House, some twenty miles away, where she had been placed in the charge of a noble lady of the court soon after her birth, so that she would not serve as a constant and galling reminder that Queen Anne Boleyn had borne her husband a daughter, instead of the son she should have provided. Six-year-old Prince Edward was at Hatfield House with her. The two were brought back to Hampton Court to receive some long-overdue mothering and affection.

King Henry, though, did not have long to enjoy the family life provided. Foreign affairs soon began to demand most of his attention, much of his time, and a good deal of his personal presence. At an age and in a physical condition that should have dictated comfort and retirement, he found himself faced with more military action than at any other time in his life. By agreement with Emperor Charles V, he would soon have to be in France, personally directing his part of the great and thus-far secret invasion which they had plotted together. While he was gone, Queen Catherine Parr would serve as regent in his stead, much as Catherine of Aragon had done during his earlier wars, five marriages before.

France was to be the first order of business, now that—as King Henry optimistically supposed—Scotland had been brought under control. The trouble was that Scotland would not stay under control. Henry had left James Hamilton, Earl of Arran, firmly in

Catherine Parr, Henry's sixth wife. (Engraving after Hans Holbein the Younger)

charge, to inch the country bit by bit from a condition of independence to one of unity with, and under, England. Now,
suddenly, there was a revolt against Arran, headed by Cardinal
Beaton and the Earl of Lennox. This was bad enough, but it
became much worse when Arran joined the revolt which had
been launched against him and turned the whole thing against
King Henry.

Henry reacted quickly against the Scottish revolt, appointing a
new man, the Earl of Angus, to head the English faction in Scotland and demanding that the Scots abandon their old allies, the
French, and show loyalty to England. The Scots refused. Henry
then sent Edward Seymour, the Earl of Hertford, across the
border with an English army. Meeting little resistance, Hertford
took and sacked the cities of Leith and Edinburgh.

At this point, King Henry had no more time or energy to
devote to Scotland. He was forced to realize that, instead of a
friendly and cooperative land, as he had supposed, Scotland was
still an ardent ally of the French and was still hostile to England.

The summer of 1544 was the time that had finally been set
for the great and secret invasion of France. When first conceived
two years before, it had had all the allure of a glorious day-
dream. With King Henry invading from the west and Emperor
Charles from the east, how could the invasion possibly fail? As
the time approached, however, there were misgivings. Charles
looked upon Henry as a monstrously fat has-been with an ulcerated leg, and Henry looked upon Charles as an old man hope-
lessly crippled with the gout. How could either ruler hope to
lead an army to any sort of victory? The only redeeming feature
was that their prospective enemy, King Francis I, was little better
off than either of them. Syphilis had robbed him of much of
whatever strength and alertness his age of fifty might have left
him.

King Henry, though two years older than King Francis, was

determined to gain military glory by leading his armies in person. By way of preparation, he had had a vast, new suit of armor made to accommodate his ever-increasing bulk, and he had a great, strong dray horse trained to carry him into battle. Many thought that this was a foolish and useless risk of his life, but he became so angry at the few who tried to dissuade him that it was not long before all such attempts ceased. The plans went ahead for the invasion under the king's personal leadership.

The first step in the war was the sending of a powerful English army to the continent under the Dukes of Suffolk and Norfolk. The landing was made at Calais, directly across the narrowest part of the Channel, the one port of mainland Europe which then belonged to England. There was no immediate move to fulfill the pledge to Emperor Charles to attack Paris from the west. Instead, the Duke of Norfolk—who always seemed to fight much better on English soil than abroad—began a listless and in-effective siege of Montreuil, near the coast some miles south of Calais. King Henry crossed to Calais on July 14, 1544, with an army of about thirty thousand men. Presently, he laid siege to the Channel port of Boulogne.

Emperor Charles, meanwhile, had been blundering his way up the Marne Valley toward Paris, in an attempt to fulfill his end of the bargain. Gradually, it became evident to him that King Henry was doing very little to cooperate. Imperial messengers, sent to the camp outside Boulogne, succeeded only in learn-ing that Henry was intent on taking that seaport before doing anything else. It seemed clear that the taking of Paris would be left to Charles, acting alone.

September 18, 1544, was a key day in the war. Two important things happened almost within the same hour: Boulogne sur-rendered to King Henry, and Emperor Charles made a separate peace with King Francis, thus leaving the French forces with only a single foe to face, England.

Almost at once, the tide of battle turned against King Henry. The siege of Montreuil had to be abandoned when a strong French army led by the Dauphin of France attacked the Duke of Norfolk from behind and threatened to trap him and his army against the walls of the city. King Henry returned to England in disgust, after instructing the Dukes of Norfolk and Suffolk to make sure that "our daughter"—Boulogne—was strongly held. The dukes, though, presently retired into Calais, leaving only a small force to hold Boulogne.

It was not only abroad that things were going badly for King Henry. While the French were gathering their forces for an attack on Boulogne and an invasion of England, Scotland struck a blow in behalf of her French allies. On February 27, 1545, a Scottish force under Archibald Douglas attacked and routed five thousand English soldiers on Ancrum Moor, thus scoring the first Scottish military victory in generations. Though it was not a major engagement, it sent a chill through England, for it raised the spectre of French landings in Scotland to be followed by a joint French-Scottish invasion of England.

The French did not send an expedition to Scotland. They had, it seemed, a more direct thought in mind. Their eyes were on Portsmouth, the only fully equipped naval base on the English Channel. It was from Portsmouth that the English garrisons at Calais and Boulogne were receiving their supplies and reinforcements. An important first step toward the taking of these two outposts would be the capture, crippling, or blockading of Portsmouth. On July 18, 1545, a formidable French fleet of 108 vessels under Admiral Claude D'Annibault crossed the Channel and approached the Portsmouth waterfront.

At the head of the French fleet were four long, narrow Mediterranean rowing galleys. As soon as these were sighted, already-prepared signal flares were lighted on the towers of Portsmouth. They were seen by watchers on the hilltops, who promptly lighted flares of their own, to alert other watchers farther inland. Within a matter of minutes, the countryside for many miles around had been alerted, and men were on the march toward the threatened naval base.

Another man on the move was King Henry VIII. He had been having dinner with his top officers aboard the *Great Harry* when the French galleys were sighted. With all speed he went over the side and was rowed ashore to organize the land defenses, while Admiral John Dudley, Lord Lisle, prepared the fleet for action. Compared to what was coming against it, it was not much of a fleet, for it included only sixty-three vessels. Not only were the English ships fewer in number; on the whole, they averaged considerably smaller than the French vessels which would be opposing them.

For the moment, though, all of the French fleet that was in sight was the little squadron of four galleys. Out of the harbor after them went fourteen sail-driven English warships. The galleys were faster, but they plied their oars just hard enough to stay ahead of their pursuers, hoping to draw the fourteen pursuers into the heart of the French fleet, lurking just over the horizon. The fourteen were not that incautious. As soon as other ships were sighted, they came about and returned to Portsmouth.

The sun arose next morning on a flat and windless sea. Under such conditions, no sailing ship could move. It was a perfect day for galley action, though, and D'Annibault sent all twenty-five of his rowing galleys to take advantage of this fact. The long, thin, fast vessels, with their rams and forward-firing guns, rowed boldly into Portsmouth harbor and attacked the anchored and becalmed English vessels.

It was a dangerous maneuver, but the French galley captains knew what they were doing and handled it well. The English ships had opened their gunports and had run out their heavy guns, ready to fire smashing broadsides into any galley that appeared alongside. The galleys, therefore, attacked from bow and stern, where the English guns that could be brought to bear were few and small. As the galleys' heavy guns all fired straight ahead, they had all the advantage in this type of fighting.

To the rescue came some quick-witted men from the navy yard. They had available a number of broad, tubby barges, known as "rowing pieces." These were not warships, being used mostly for the transportation of supplies about the harbor. They were quickly armed with a variety of light cannons and were sent out against the French war galleys. It was a strange contest. The "rowing pieces" were much smaller and very much slower than the galleys, and their guns were less powerful. They had two advantages, though. They were much more maneuverable, and their guns could be moved to fire in any direction. When some of the galleys began to show signs of damage, the entire squadron of twenty-five retired from the harbor.

Scarcely had the galleys gone when a breeze sprang up. Lord Lisle ordered sails up, moorings slipped, and the French galleys pursued and destroyed. Almost at once, disaster struck. Aboard the *Mary Rose*, second largest of the English ships, someone had forgotten to order the guns run in and the gunports closed, after the French withdrew. Now, as the great vessel began to heel with the wind, the starboard gun deck rolled beneath the surface. Water poured in, and the warship sank like a stone, leaving few survivors. The pursuit of the French was called off.

Truly, *Mary Rose* was a jinx name for English warships!

The French were not quite ready to go home. Their fleet dropped anchor off the English Isle of Wight, and a landing force was sent ashore. They were armed with the very latest of weapons—the muzzle-loading, flintlock musket. It was a noisy and terrifying device, and great things were expected of it. The English defenders, on the other hand, had only their trusty longbows with which to resist the French.

The results were surprising. Once the English bowmen had

become accustomed to the noisy new weapons in the hands of the Frenchmen, they found that they themselves had many advantages. When a musketeer had fired his piece, he was helpless until he had completed a long and involved reloading process. While this was happening, a bowman could discharge a number of arrows, each as capable of killing a man as was the slug from a noisy musket. The Frenchmen were driven out.

Presently, the same thing happened farther east, at Seaford, where D'Annibault tried another invasion. This time, there was an added feature. While the musketeers were being beaten on the shore, the French fleet had blundered into a dangerous situation. Near their anchorage was a deadly, hidden shoal called The Owers. Hoping that a sudden attack would cause the French to slip their moorings and run onto the rocks, Admiral Lisle led his English ships toward the French position. Only the sudden dying out of the wind prevented the attack from being carried through.

King Henry was furious at his admiral for having attacked without the royal permission. Lord Lisle received a thorough dressing down and was made to understand that another such incident might cost him his head. As a result, when the French fleet finally withdrew and a good opportunity for an attack presented itself, the admiral did nothing. D'Annibault retired to France unmolested.

The experience with the "rowing pieces" in Portsmouth harbor led to a valuable addition to the English fleet. A squadron of galleasses was secured and placed under the command of Captain William Tyrell. These were large, three-masted galleys, armed with cannons bearing in all directions and equipped with sails for use when there was a wind and with oars for use when there was not. They had been specifically developed in the Mediterranean area to counter the use of galleys, such as those with D'Annibault's fleet.

The French came again in August and were met in mid-

Channel by Lisle's warships. The wind was much too light to permit effective maneuvering by the sailing vessels of either fleet. D'Annibault therefore sent his galleys out to attack the handicapped English warships. Lisle countered with Tyrell's galleass squadron, slower but able to fire in all directions. The results were not decisive, but favored the English, for the French galleys were heavily battered and were kept away from the English sailing ships. As darkness fell, both fleets dropped anchor, presumably to wait out the hours of darkness and resume the battle in the morning, when the wind might be much better. The wind came up before the sun, and when daylight dawned the French anchorage was empty. D'Annibault had gone home. He did not come back.

Both nations were discouraged by a war that seemed to be accomplishing very little for either one. In June 1546, Emperor Charles accepted the role of mediator in a peace conference. After much hard bargaining, it was agreed that King Henry would restore Boulogne to the French in 1554, provided the French had by that time paid him a "ransom" of two million crowns. When that agreement had been reached, nothing stood in the way of the second provision of the treaty, that England, France, and Scotland should immediately cease fighting. They did.

King Henry's foresight in building up his fleet had saved England from a dangerous invasion and quite possibly from a French conquest. Now, with the war over, he did not let his navy decay and disappear. A new branch of the government was set up to supervise the building, equipment, maintenance, and supply of warships. From that time on, England was a formidable naval power, well able to hold its own with the other powers of the world.

A few words should be said about the part which Catherine Parr played in the war, for it brings sharply to mind the participation of Catherine of Aragon in those earlier wars against

Scotland and France. When King Henry set out for the Continent in the summer of 1544, he appointed his new bride Governor of the Realm and Protector during his absence. She worked hard to live up to the imposing title, writing frequent reports of conditions at home and keeping him well informed. While she could not, like Henry's able and energetic first wife, issue the orders which led directly to a military victory over Scottish invaders, her letters had a strong, though indirect, bearing on the outcome of the war. One, for example, informed him of the capture of a Scottish ship bearing French representatives and supplies for a possible northern invasion. Such information was vital to the king.

It has become customary to think of Catherine Parr as the colorless last wife who nursed King Henry through his final years. Such a designation is by no means fair. She was, in many ways, a great deal more than that.

# 13
# KING HENRY'S FINAL MONTHS

THE treaty with France, unsatisfactory though it seemed at the time, marked the end of King Henry's foreign wars. From this time on, the problems faced would be largely religious in nature.

It was a time of religious rivalries, some over great issues, more over minor variations in doctrine. King Henry himself described his clergy in these words: "Some are so stiff in their old *mumpsimus*, and others so busy with their new *sumpsimus*" that they do nothing but criticize one another while the laymen debate religious questions in the taverns and alehouses.

These strange terms had their origin in an amusing true story that was circulating around England at the time. It seems that there was an old priest who, for most of his life, had been misreading a Latin word in his prayer book, saying *mumpsimus*, when it should have been *sumpsimus*. When someone at last pointed out his error, he grew very angry and declared, "I will never change my old *mumpsimus* for your new *sumpsimus!*" It made an excellent way for King Henry to characterize the many unimportant differences that were then causing ill feeling between the Catholic-favoring and Protestant-favoring branches of his new English Church.

King Henry's lack of regard for the common people of his realm is well shown by a law which he compelled Parliament to pass limiting ownership or reading of the Bible to nobles and gentlemen. The purpose was to keep "people of the lower sort" from getting troublesome ideas and from trying to reshape religious beliefs on the basis of some of the tavern and alehouse arguments. One such man, for example, had become widely known for having come upon a passage in the Bible which apparently permitted a husband to have more than one wife, so he had promptly married a second one while still keeping his first!

Religious doctrine even assumed an undue importance in King Henry's dealings with the Pope and with foreign heads of state. Being perched, as it were, in the middle of the seesaw, between the Catholics on one end and the extreme Protestants on the other, he was able to influence members of either group by a slight shift of weight. In general, this activity took the form of harsh condemnation and often execution of Protestant extremists during his negotiations with Catholics, and of Catholics when dealing with Protestants.

In the summer of 1546, Pope Paul III sent a trusted emissary, Guron Bertano, to submit a tempting proposal to King Henry. The Pope offered to give official Church approval to Henry's divorce from Catherine of Aragon, to his seizure of the Catholic monasteries in England, and to certain other acts which the Church had not accepted. In exchange, King Henry was officially to accept and admit the Pope's supremacy in all religious matters. Henry was strongly tempted. For one thing, this agreement would permit him to remove the taint of illegitimacy from thirty-year-old Princess Mary, a taint which had thus far kept her from getting a husband. For another, it would give him a permanent and unquestionable right to the millions of dollars' worth of property which he had taken from the Church for his own use. Yes, he would gain, but he would also have to give, and King Henry of England was not accustomed to giving much in exchange for what he received. In the end he rejected the Pope's offer.

Close association with King Henry VIII was never safe, no matter how much power one had been granted or how much one appeared to be in favor. An important reason for this was the strong division within the King's Council. The rival Council members were not above using false witnesses to discredit and destroy those who were in a position to block their activities, and the king was not always above accepting what he must have known or suspected to be invented evidence. We have already seen what he had permitted in the cases of Cardinal Wolsey and Thomas Cromwell, and there were scores of lesser people similarly removed while the king intentionally looked in the other direction.

There were times, however, when King Henry surprised those who were counting on him to avert his eyes and permit a liquidation. A few such situations are worth examining in some detail.

Stephen Gardiner, Bishop of Winchester and for many years one of King Henry's close associates, had a nephew named Germayne Gardiner, who also served as his secretary. Germayne was a religious conservative, for he continued to believe that the Pope, rather than the king, should be the head of the English Church. In 1544, Germayne Gardiner expressed himself a bit too positively on this ticklish question. His enemies in the Council, led by Charles Brandon, Duke of Suffolk, brought charges against him, and he was quickly seized and beheaded. This same group of Council members were also enemies of the bishop, and it seemed to them an excellent opportunity to get rid of the uncle as well as the nephew. The charge was made that Germayne would not have dared to proclaim his treasonous doctrine so loudly and positively unless he was counting on the bishop's backing. Papers were prepared for the arrest and execution of Stephen Gardiner. Someone sent word to the bishop, though, and he managed to get to the king and to reestablish himself in

His Majesty's good graces. When a group came to serve the papers and arrest Bishop Gardiner, the king furiously sent them on their way.

Two years later, in 1546, Bishop Gardiner again found himself in serious trouble for lack of enthusiasm in surrendering some fine lands in his diocese in exchange for some inferior lands that the king wished to get rid of. Once more, unfriendly Council members moved to arrest him, and once more the bishop learned of it in time to flee to the king, though this time he had more trouble in reaching His Majesty. In the end, the king saved him again, but the two incidents together had raised some strong doubts in Henry's mind concerning Stephen Gardiner, Bishop of Winchester.

In 1545, between Gardiner's two close brushes with death, something rather similar happened to Archbishop Cranmer. The country was excited about heresy, and officials were kept busy sniffing out those whose beliefs differed ever so slightly from those held by the king and his officials of Church and State. Once taken, such a heretic was almost certain to be burned at the stake. One of the leading bloodhounds in the suppression of heresy was the Lord Chancellor of England, Sir Thomas Wriothesley, Earl of Southampton. Wriothesley and some of his associates, objecting to Cranmer's mildness on the subject of heresy, drew up a paper stating that "the primate, with his learned men, has so infected the whole realm with unsavory doctrine as to fill all places with abominable heretics." Not only the Church was in danger, they wrote, but the very throne itself. King Henry summoned the authors of the paper and asked what they would recommend. They urged sending Archbishop Cranmer to the Tower. The King felt that this was too strong a punishment, but he did agree to have them summon Cranmer before the Council and question him. If the questioning seemed to establish guilt, *then* he could be sent to the Tower.

That evening, King Henry fretted about the situation. He was fond of Archbishop Cranmer and had frequently found him very useful. Finally, though the hour was late, he summoned Cranmer to him. As the archbishop arrived, Henry glanced at the paper in his hand, smiled, and said, "Ah, My Lord Archbishop. I now know who is the greatest heretic in Kent." Cranmer looked surprised and asked who it was. King Henry told him, "It is you," then informed him of the charges made in the paper. Cranmer was not excited, but declared that he could easily prove his innocence.

The king goggled at him. "Oh, Lord God!" he cried "What fond simplicity have you so to permit yourself to be imprisoned, that every enemy of yours may take advantage against you! Do you not know that when they have you once in prison, three or four false knaves will soon be procured to witness against you and condemn you?" Then, having clearly shown that he knew precisely how "justice" was administered in his realm, the king gave Cranmer his ring and told him to make use of it if he found himself in trouble.

The trouble was not long in coming. The very next day, the archbishop was summoned to appear before the Council. When told he was charged with heresy, he demanded to meet his accusers and hear from their lips what they had to say against him. This was refused. At that, he sighed and said, "I am sorry, My Lords, that you drive me to such a step, but seeing myself likely to obtain no fair usage from you, I must appeal to His Majesty." With that, he produced King Henry's ring. The meaning was clear, but the affair had gone too far to be quietly dropped. The accusing lords took the papers and the ring to King Henry, who criticized them severely for the action they had taken against the archbishop. One of the accusers stammered that their only purpose had been to give Archbishop Cranmer an opportunity to disprove the charges made against him—a statement which deceived nobody. The king insisted that they drop the charges and shake hands with Archbishop Cranmer, which they all did.

Not all heretics were men. Women, too, dabbled in the then-dangerous game of discussing and spreading religious beliefs, and some of these were made to suffer for it. One of the unhappiest was Anne Askew, of Lincolnshire. She and her husband had originally been staunch Catholics, but as she discussed religion with various people some of her beliefs changed so strongly that her more conservative husband drove her away from her home, from him, and from their two children. She went to London, where she was accused of heresy, imprisoned, and sentenced to die by fire. It had been said that she had gained her heretical ideas by association with some prominent people, and her judges wanted to get their names. She refused to give any. She was placed on the rack and tortured dreadfully, but still she would not speak. When her jailers refused to torture her further, Sir Thomas Wriothesley and Sir Richard Rich stepped forth and operated the machine themselves, subjecting her to increased agony. Still, she would not speak, and they were denied the evidence they sought. On July 16, 1546—still so badly injured by the rack that she could neither walk nor stand—she was carried to Smithfield on a chair and there was burned to death.

Though Anne Askew had refused to give any names, one very prominent name had been associated with her at her trial. Among the charges made was one that she had delivered heretical books and pamphlets to Catherine Parr, wife of King Henry VIII!

There was a certain amount of logic in this, for Queen Catherine was much interested in religious questions and enjoyed discussing them with any who would listen, including King Henry himself. As she became more deeply involved, she began to hold classes in Scripture for her ladies-in-waiting. One of her pet projects was the further reform of the Church of England, to move it still further from the strict teachings of the Catholic Church. With increasing frequency, she strongly urged upon King Henry the reforms she wished. His ulcerated leg was suffering, his health was bad, and he could no longer escape her lectures easily nor endure them as peacefully as he had.

Bishop Gardiner saw in this situation a chance to strike down "this dangerous female heretic," whom he did not trust. Accordingly, he went to the King and criticized Queen Catherine, offering to work with other members of the Council to draw up charges of treason and heresy so strong and so precise that "His Majesty will easily perceive how perilous a matter it is to cherish a serpent within his own bosom."

King Henry gave the bishop permission to draw up the charges, and when he had read them over he consented to sign them. At this point, it looked as though another royal wife was headed for destruction. One must conclude, though, that the king had his own purposes in mind rather than Bishop Gardiner's. A few days later, a member of the Council "accidentally" dropped from the front of his doublet a formal-looking paper, which happened to land at the feet of one of the queen's ladies-in-waiting. She promptly snatched it up and bore it directly to her mistress. Queen Catherine read the document with growing horror, for it contained charges of heresy directed at her by name and at three of her ladies-in-waiting. When she came to the end and saw that the king had signed it, she fell in a dead faint. When she recovered consciousness, she was so ill that she had to retire to her bed.

Hearing of his wife's illness, King Henry went to her room. She said she feared she had offended him and begged him to pardon her if she had. He said nothing about being offended, and they talked for quite some time in a friendly manner before the king departed.

Another visitor arrived—Dr. John Wendy, one of the king's physicians. After determining that the queen was not seriously ill, he confided to her that she would be in no danger if only she would assure the king that she would no longer discuss her religious ideas with him or with others. It is presumed that the king had told Wendy to reveal this in the greatest confidence, as though the doctor were risking his very life by telling her. It is also presumed that the dropping of the papers and their prompt snatching up and delivery had been carefully planned beforehand.

Catherine Parr, being a woman of intelligence, very quickly did just the right thing. She visited the king in his room and asked his forgiveness for whatever she had done. He hesitated, then asked her a question dealing with religion. She declined to answer, saying that it would not be fitting for a wife to direct her husband's thinking, but that she should be guided by "Your Majesty's wisdom, as my only anchor, supreme head and governor here in earth, next under God, to lean upon."

"Not so, by St. Mary!" said the king. "You are become a doctor, Kate, to instruct us—as we take it—and not to be instructed or directed by us."

Very earnestly, Queen Catherine denied that she had been trying to instruct her husband. She had talked religion to him only to help him keep his mind from his painful, ulcerated leg and to learn the real truth from his answers. For her to try to instruct him—the King and the Head of the Church—would be preposterous. Never again, she said, would she presume to discuss points of religion.

"And is it even so, Sweetheart?" said King Henry kindly. "Then perfect friends we are now again as ever at any time heretofore."

The next day, King Henry sent word that the queen and the three ladies-in-waiting named in the paper should join him in the garden. Not long after they arrived, the gate opened, and in strode Lord Chancellor Wriothesley with forty armed men. He had come, he said, to take the four women to the Tower. King Henry flew into a rage. "Knave!" he shouted at Wriothese-ley, "Fool! Beast! Knave! Arrant knave! Fool! Avaunt from my presence!"

Wriothesley dropped abjectly to his knees before his king, who continued to berate him. Queen Catherine, tenderhearted as ever, hurried over to intercede. The king turned to her. "Ah, poor soul," he said, "thou little knowest how evil he hath de-served this grace at thy hands. On my word, Sweetheart, he hath been toward thee an arrant knave, and so let him go."

Wriothesley, at that point, was more than glad to take his men and to depart. He had, indeed, been in on the plot, but the mastermind behind the attempt to execute Queen Catherine had been Bishop Gardiner. From this point on, the bishop was for-bidden to approach the king, and presently his name was stricken from the list of those who would guide Prince Edward when he should succeed his father, as King Edward VI.

As the year 1546 drew toward its end, it became increasingly evident that it would not be long until England would have a new ruler. The King's ulcerated leg grew weaker and more pain-ful, and the ulcer itself became a nauseous sight. The king was a slowly dying man, but no one dared tell him, for all remem-bered Walter, Lord Hungerford, who had been put to death in 1540 for incorrectly foretelling King Henry's death on the occa-sion of one of his earlier serious illnesses. So life at Hampton Court went on much as before, though the pace grew slower and slower and the king's appearances in public briefer and rarer.

As the seriousness of the king's illness became more and more evident, members of the king's Council and others became in-creasingly interested in the guidance of Prince Edward, when he should become the boy-king, Edward VI. This was a question which bore a heavy cargo of mutual jealousy, of trouble, and for one family, at least, of downright tragedy.

Thomas Howard, Duke of Norfolk, had a thirty-year-old son named Henry Howard, Earl of Surrey, whom we have already met as "the poet Surrey." The Howards had royal blood in their veins, being directly descended from the Plantagenet family which ruled England from 1154 through 1485.

The Duke of Norfolk, though personally unpopular with a great many influential people in England, had served King Henry long and faithfully. He may have confided to his son his hopes about increased influence when Edward VI should have the throne; if he did, he was foolish, for Surrey, in addition to being a brilliant poet, was also a loudmouthed braggart and roisterer who showed no discretion at all in the things he said aloud. In the alehouses with his friends, he boasted of his royal blood and showed a new royal coat of arms which he had designed, including his own family symbols. He also said that he had urged his own sister to catch the king's eye and become his last mistress. He predicted that when the king should die, his father, the Duke of Norfolk, would be the one who would guide young Edward. Not all of the ears to which these boasts came belonged to people who were friendly to the House of Howard.

King Henry lay on his deathbed, but he roused himself for final action when a three-man committee, including Edward Seymour, Earl of Hertford; John Dudley, Viscount Lisle; and Archbishop Cranmer appeared before him, told him of the things that Surrey had been saying, and added the opinion that the Duke of Norfolk was the real guilty party, urging on his son. It is worth noting that a memeber of the committee was Edward Seymour, an uncle of the Prince, who had been expecting to exercise some influence in his own behalf over the fledgling King Edward VI.

To King Henry, the news must have looked like a direct assault on all his well-laid plans. Orders were issued: first Surrey, then Norfolk, was seized and taken to the Tower. At his trial, the poet summoned his mastery of the language in his own defense and briefly seemed to be swaying his judges. It was in vain. A quiet word from the royal sickroom brought a verdict of guilty. Norfolk, at his trial, expressed shock and amazement, citing his many services to the king and insisting that he had never conspired. Perhaps he had not, but he had aspired, and that was enough to convict him of treason. Both men were sentenced to death by beheading, the son's execution to take place on January 19, the father's on January 28.

From time to time, during the final month of 1546, King Henry had roused himself sufficiently to attend brief meetings of his Council. He could no longer walk, but had to be carried from room to room of the palace in a heavy sedan chair, especially designed to support his enormous weight. With the coming of the New Year, such excursions were no longer possible. Now, he was confined to the sickroom, never again to leave it. It must have been a dreadful place for him and for those who attended him. The two princesses were told not to come and see him, because of the disgusting odors from his ulcerated leg. Nothing like this, however, could keep Queen Catherine from doing her best to ease the ebbing life of her sick husband.

Word came on January 19 that Surrey had been executed. The king showed little interest. An appeal for mercy was received from the condemned Duke of Norfolk, but King Henry would do nothing in his behalf.

Although no one—doctor or courtier—had dared to tell him, King Henry surely knew by mid-January that he was dying. He had already had his will read aloud to him and had dictated some minor changes in it. Now, despite the stench of the sickroom, he sent, one at a time, for the princesses and for Queen Catherine.

First he saw Mary, his thirty-year-old daughter by Catherine of Aragon. He spoke sadly of the fact that he had never secured a husband for her, though he did not mention the fact that it was his insistence on her illegitimacy that had been the principal cause of his failure. He then added, "I pray thee, my daughter, try to be a mother to thy brother, for, look, he is little yet." When Mary started to weep, he dismissed her.

Next came thirteen-year-old Elizabeth, his daughter by Anne Boleyn. She, too, was weeping and was soon told to leave.

To Queen Catherine he said, "It is God's will that we should part, and I order all these gentlemen to honor you and treat you as if I were living still." He told her that he had just added the name of Thomas Seymour to the Council, and he assured her that after he was gone he wanted her to keep the jewels and other items he had left her. She, too, wept and soon departed.

Steadily, hour by hour, the king lost strength. Dangerous or not, someone had to tell him that his time was coming fast. Sir Anthony Denny, the king's "gentleman of the chamber," volunteered to do it, and he did, on the evening of January 27, 1547.

King Henry took the news of his approaching death calmly. He whispered to Denny that although he had sinned, "yet is the mercy of Christ able to pardon all my sins, though they were greater than they be."

Denny asked if there were not some man of the Church to whom he would like to confess. King Henry paused, then said, "Cranmer, but he not yet." At that, King Henry drifted off to sleep.

Little by little, the king's sleep turned into an unconscious state from which he could never completely emerge. Word was sent to Archbishop Cranmer, who hurried to the bedside. King Henry was still alive, his great body propped up on his bed, his eyes unfocused, staring, seeing nothing. He could not speak, could not raise his hand or his head. Cranmer knelt beside the bed and took his sovereign's huge, thick, powerless hand in his. Speaking slowly, distinctly, and very earnestly, the archbishop asked a most important question: "Do you die in the faith of Christ?"

King Henry could not answer, though his eyes stared and his breath wheezed in his lungs. Briefly, the churchman continued to kneel at the bedside, his hand clasped with the king's. Then he released his hold, stood up, and announced to those gathered about the bed that the king was indeed dying in the faith of Christ, for when asked the question "he did wring my hand as hard as he could."

Not many minutes later—at about two o'clock in the morning of January 28, 1547—the struggle was over, and King Henry VIII of England was dead.

# 14
# A QUESTION OF SUCCESSION

OR no one were the results of King Henry's death more immediate or more important than for Thomas Howard, Duke of Norfolk. January 28, 1547, was to have been the day of his execution. For some strange reason, the attendants did not come early to his cell to lead him out to the block for his appointment with the headsman's axe. As he paced the floor in anxious uncertainty, the duke did not know that the king had died at two o'clock that morning and that no one yet knew what to do about a man sentenced to death by a king who no longer reigned or even lived.

Normally, when a ruler dies, bells are tolled, flags fly at half-staff, and the cry is heard, "The King is dead! Long live the King!" This time, there was only silence for three days. The death was kept a secret while the Council members debated, first what to do with the Duke of Norfolk, then how the terms of the king's will should be carried out. Only when agreement had been reached on both questions were the English people told that Henry VIII had died and they had a new king, Edward VI.

The duke's life was spared, but he was not released. It was finally decided to hold him a prisoner in the Tower indefinitely, which, in effect, meant for the remaining seven years of his life.

King Edward VI came to the throne as a pudgy, unhealthy boy of nine. According to the late king's will, important decisions were to be made for him by a Council of Executors, named in

Edward VI, King of England from 1547 to 1553. (Portrait by an unknown artist)

the will. Chief among these was the new king's uncle, Edward Seymour, Earl of Hertford, who now received a new and higher title, Duke of Somerset, and a string of designations which effectively put him at the head of the government: "governor of His Majesty, lord-protector of all His realms, lieutenant-general of all His armies." In justification of this quiet assumption of supreme power, the new Duke of Somerset maintained that he had received letters from the late King Henry appointing him to the rights and duties involved.

Though the new king was far too young to rule, he showed many kingly qualities. He studied unceasingly the subjects which his tutors felt he would later need—languages, history, geography, government, and military-naval topics. Archbishop Cranmer's teachings had made him far more of a Protestant than his father, whose balance between Protestant and Catholic extremes had kept him near the middle of the road. Edward took his royal status very seriously. No one was permitted to approach him without first kneeling abjectly before him; this applied even to his royal sisters, Mary and Elizabeth.

Under Cranmer's guidance, and with the strong backing of Lord-Protector Edward Seymour, the English Church swung steadily toward the Protestant end of the seesaw. The archbishop himself set a precedent by publicly eating meat during Lent. Sermons, which had played small part in the Catholic services, gained steadily in numbers and importance. Some of the subjects were even prescribed. The Mass, in fact, was presently forbidden; even strongly Catholic Princess Mary was permitted to practice it only in the privacy of her own rooms. In 1549, there was an uprising in western England by people who wanted their Church services in Latin, as before, instead of in English. Instead of putting down the trouble by force of arms, Archbishop Cranmer went to the spot and made a speech: "The priest is your proctor and attorney, to plead your cause and to speak for you all. Had you rather not know than know what he saieth for you? I have heard suitors murmur at the bar, because their attorneys were pleading their cases in the French tongue, which they understood not. Why, then, be you offended that the priests, who plead your cause before God, should speak such language as you may understand?" The speech had the effect desired. The uprising died.

From time to time we have encountered Edward and Thomas Seymour, the energetic brothers of King Henry's third queen, Jane Seymour. As Jane was the mother of King Edward VI, the Seymour brothers were the new king's uncles, a fact which should have guaranteed both of them important posts in the government.

Indeed, the new regime started out profitably for both brothers. Edward, Duke of Somerset, as we have seen, succeeded in establishing himself as Lord-Protector, the Number One man in the government until the boy-king should come of age. Thomas, the younger brother, also rose in power and in honors after King Henry's death, gaining the title of Baron Sudeley and becoming Lord High Admiral of the English fleet. If they had worked well together, as brothers often do, there would have been almost no limit to the heights they might have reached. They did not do so.

We must remember that when King Henry first set eyes on Catherine Parr and decided to make her his sixth queen, she was being courted by Tom Seymour. They were not yet formally engaged to be married, and Seymour wisely stepped aside, leaving the field clear for the king. Now that King Henry was dead, Tom Seymour quickly returned, and soon he and Queen-Dowager Catherine Parr were married.

The marriage brought on a bitter and damaging rivalry between the brothers. Edward Seymour's status as Lord-Protector made him the highest ranking official in the kingdom, except for the boy-king himself. As the king was not married, the

Lord-Protector's wife, Anne Stanhope, had been enjoying the highest female social position in the kingdom. When the marriage of Tom Seymour and Queen-Dowager Catherine Parr was revealed, Anne Stanhope's social supremacy was threatened. Bitterly, she insisted that as the wife of the highest official she outranked even the former queen. The rivalry between the Seymour wives very quickly drove a wedge between the brothers.

Thomas Seymour was not above driving a few wedges of his own. He had long had a rakish and unsavory reputation, especially as regards women, and he rather quickly showed that it was well earned. It is said that before he married Catherine Parr he had tried to win the hand, first of Princess Mary, then of Princess Elizabeth. Mary had had no use for him at all, and Elizabeth, at fourteen, had been a bit too young for marriage. Now, still under the care of Catherine Parr, as she had been before King Henry's death, she had to live in the same house with a man who harbored some rather doubtful ambitions concerning her.

Catherine Parr found herself in a most unhappy situation. She was pregnant, having become so almost as soon as she had married Seymour. This placed her at a double disadvantage, for her increasing awkwardness and bulkiness made it more difficult to compete with Anne Stanhope for social standing and with the various women who took her husband's eye, including young Princess Elizabeth.

Things were in this unhappy state when Catherine Parr suddenly fell ill and died. It is believed that her fatal illness arose from her pregnancy, being associated with a difficult childbirth or a miscarriage, but at the time it was suspected that her husband had grown tired of her, or more interested in the princess, and had managed to get rid of her by means of poison.

Tom Seymour behaved no better after his wife's death. Unpleasant stories of many sorts circulated about him, and a few of these led to formal legal charges. For example, it was said that he was in league with bands of pirates, letting them know where the units of the fleet would be at certain times, so that they could operate safely somewhere else, and receiving for his help a share of their loot. He was said to be seeking the hand of Princess Elizabeth, without gaining the permission of the Council, as provided by the late king's will. It was even whispered that he was planning to abduct the boy-king, Edward, and hold him until he should give permission for such a marriage.

Distressing as these rumors were, something far worse was soon to come. Early in 1549, the master of the royal mint at Bristol was arrested for debasing the currency—using cheap metals instead of gold and silver for the making of certain valuable coins. This man saved his own life by implicating the Lord High Admiral as the man responsible for having him do it. Formal charges were brought against Thomas Seymour, who was promptly arrested and thrust into the Tower.

It is often dangerous to bring such a man as Seymour to trial. As the evidence comes forth, other names may be mentioned and other people charged. The prosecution avoided all this by holding no trial. No witnesses were examined. The defense was not permitted to offer any evidence in behalf of the prisoner. Instead, Parliament passed one of those convenient bills of attainder, declaring Thomas Seymour guilty. A few days later, a warrant was issued, providing for his execution. The first of the many signatures on the warrant was that of his brother, Edward Seymour.

Tom Seymour's head was separated from his body in March 20, 1549.

The year 1549 was a dreadful time for many others in England, besides Thomas Seymour. Underlying discontents surfaced, and violence and bloodshed broke out in numerous, widely separated places. There were many reasons. Perhaps the commonest was the heartfelt desire of the country people to have the old Catholic religious ceremonies restored.

Another source of discontent was the enclosure of what had been public lands. Crops had been raised on these lands by farmers too poor to own lands of their own—crops which had supplied food and even a little money income to the families of the peasant-farmers. Now, in area after area, the former public lands were being claimed and fenced in by wealthy aristocrats who wanted to use them for raising sheep, to supply wool to the growing clothing industry. The poor people were being kept from the lands they had once used; their manner of living was being ruined.

A third unpopular activity was the debasing of the currency, in much the same way that it had been done by the master of the Bristol mint. Money dropped in value, requiring ever larger amounts for the purchase of supplies and the paying of debts. Everybody suffered some, but it was the poor who suffered most.

During the spring months of 1549, there were six minor peasant uprisings in the rural areas of England. None was very serious, though a few people were killed as the disturbances were being put down. Then, in July, a really dangerous revolt broke out in Cornwall, in the extreme southwestern corner of England. The leader was an educated gentleman named Humphrey Arundel. Lord William Russell, who was given the task of putting down the revolt, was well aware that he did not have enough troops for the purpose. Instead of rushing blindly into disastrous action, he negotiated with the rebels, promising something, anything, in order to gain time for reinforcements to arrive. They did so, at last—an English army and two mercenary groups hired abroad, one from Italy, the other from Germany.

The arrival of his reinforcements permitted Russell to cease negotiating and start fighting. Quickly, he moved to the town of Exeter, which had been under siege by the rebels. Russell broke the siege and drove the attackers away with heavy losses. Arundel's insurrection was smashed. The leader and a few of his chief assistants were captured and taken to London, where they were presently tried and executed. Most of the peasant rebels who had survived the fighting were permitted to return to their homes. .

The suppression of Arundel's revolt did not bring an end to the violence of 1549. In Norfolk, in the "bustle" of eastern England, a tanner named Robert Ket gathered the angry and discontented peasants and organized them into an army of twenty thousand men. Ket must have been a remarkable man, for he kept order among his motley followers and managed to administer justice with a fair hand. Seated under "the Oak Tree of Reformation," as he called it, this self-styled "King of Norfolk and Suffolk" held court and issued orders. The great manor houses were raided, and the enclosed lands were stripped of their cattle, sheep, swine, and poultry to feed Ket's hungry followers. Sheep were the favorite food, for they were not only good to eat but were also the principal cause of the loss of the common lands by the peasants.

Ket's revolt proved extremely troublesome to Lord-Protector Edward Seymour, Duke of Somerset. He had had sympathy for Arundel, and he had even more for Ket. It was, however, his duty as Lord-Protector to suppress such uprisings, so he sent the Marquess of Northampton with a strong army to occupy Norwich, which was serving as Ket's headquarters. To everyone's amazement, the Marquess was defeated, his army driven back with heavy losses.

As Somerset had no other local forces to send, he was compelled to call home an army which was serving in Scotland under John Dudley, the Earl of Warwick. It was an unhappy choice to have to make, for Warwick was a rival of Somerset's and was also the son of Henry VII's hated tax collector Edmund

Dudley, whom King Henry VIII had put to death early in his reign. This was a man whom the Lord-Protector would much rather have kept under cover.

The Earl of Warwick moved fast and surefootedly in putting down Ket's rebellion. A surprise attack captured Norwich and cut the rebels off from their main stores of supplies. Driven by hunger, Ket's men attacked and were defeated, with a loss of thirty-five hundred men. The survivors erected a palisade for protection and were prepared to sell their lives dearly, but when Warwick offered a general pardon, they surrendered. Robert Ket, his younger brother, and nine other leaders were hanged, but the others were all permitted to go free. Ket's rebellion was at last over.

While the revolts and rivalries were causing trouble in England, a long but intermittent war was being carried on between the English and the Scots, who were sometimes aided by their allies, the French, and more often were not.

The basic cause of the war was the deaths, in quick succession, of King Henry VIII of England and King Francis I of France. Shortly before his death, King Henry had been working to achieve peace with France, through treaty, and both peace and union with Scotland, through the marriage of Prince Edward to the infant Mary, Queen of Scots. There had seemed an excellent chance that the treaty with France would be accepted, since both King Henry and King Francis had favored it, but the new French King, Henry II, refused to ratify it. He preferred to stir up the Scots against the English and then to aid them in war.

The English-Scottish War began in 1547—the year King Henry VIII died—and ended three years later, in 1550. Though the English won the first big battle, at Pinkie, on September 10, 1547, the heavy losses by the Scots merely served to make them fight harder. Helped by the French, by some hired German mercenary troops, and by the English revolts of 1549, the Scots more than made up for their early losses. At last, in March of 1550, the Duke of Somerset had to sign a humiliating peace treaty restoring Boulogne to France for only one fifth of the ransom which King Henry VIII had originally set, abandoning the ancient claim of English kings to the throne of France, and giving up young King Edward's claim to the hand of Mary, Queen of Scots—a marriage which would have led, in time, to English possession of the Scottish throne and of Scotland itself.

It was the signing of this treaty, following the unsuccessful war and the weakly handled revolts of 1549, which led to the overthrow of Edward Seymour, Duke of Somerset, and his replacement as the chief power behind the throne by John Dudley, Earl of Warwick, who was soon to receive the higher title, Duke of Northumberland. As Warwick was rising in power, Somerset continued going down. In 1552, he was accused of plotting an armed revolt against the government and was executed.

We must remember that Edward VI, the new King of England, was still only a boy of thirteen, much too young to rule for himself. The Duke of Northumberland, backed by the Council, made the decisions for him. This was a great deal of power to place in the hands of any one man, no matter how able he might be. King Edward, though, needed someone on whom to lean. He was a pleasant, honest, kindhearted boy— one who would never intentionally harm or distress anyone. It was his misfortune that he found himself in the hands of rogues and that, as his health declined, he was forced to depend more and more on decisions made in his name.

Some of the decisions were dreadful, especially those concerning religion. In the days of King Henry VIII, there had been a fairly even balance between the extremes of the Catholic and Protestant beliefs, with people at both ends being persecuted nearly equally by the king. Now, the Protestants were in power, and most of the punishment was being dealt out to Catholics.

It took real courage to oppose those in power, but it some-times happened. To make it easier to get rid of political op-ponents, the Duke of Northumberland proposed an exceptionally vicious law against treason. England had never before seen a law which made it so easy to convict and execute opponents. Almost anything said or done to check those running the gov-ernment could be construed as treasonous. The House of Lords quickly passed the measure, lest its members be accused of treason for not doing so. The House of Commons, though, was made of sterner stuff. Its members had seen too much injustice. The law was eventually passed, but changes were written in forbidding a conviction for treason unless two witnesses of the same act agreed in their testimony and swore to it in the presence of the accused person, at his trial. This considerably reduced the abuse of power and the misuse of the treason law. It also made national heroes of the members of the House of Commons who had insisted on the changes.

As King Edward's health grew steadily worse and it became more and more evident that he had not long to live, the Duke of Northumberland began to worry. There was going to be trouble when the boy-king died. His father, King Henry VIII, had set up a royal order of succession by which Edward was to get the crown first, then Princess Mary, followed by Princess Elizabeth, and after them the children of King Henry's sister, the former Queen Mary of France. Of course, the chances were very poor of all these people coming to the throne. If Edward should live long enough to marry and to have children, then his family would follow him, and his sisters and his cousins would not. If Mary or Elizabeth should become queen, should marry, and should have children, then her family would follow. Only if all three should die childless would the little French cousins take over the crown of England, but day by day this was getting to seem more likely.

The duke's principal worry was about Princess Mary, who was

next in line after Edward. She was a very ardent Catholic, and in recent years she had been made to suffer for her religion. If she came to the throne, it seemed clear that her government would throw out the present Protestant religion and restore the Catholic faith as the official form of belief. Overnight, the persecuted Catholics would become the persecutors, and those who had been punishing Catholics for their beliefs would be the first victims in a new wave of religious savagery. He, the Duke of Northumberland, appeared likely to be among the very first.

There seemed to be only one chance of avoiding the general bloodletting that loomed ahead. That was to change the order of succession that King Henry had set up. If one king could set up one order, could not the next king set up a different one? There seemed no reason why he could not.

At the duke's urging, and following his recommendations, King Edward VI drew up a new and very different order of succession. Gone completely from the list were Princess Mary and Princess Elizabeth. King Henry had declared them both illegitimate, and Parliament had supported him.

Who, then, should follow King Edward on the throne? Why, one of the grandchildren of King Henry's sister, the former Queen Mary of France, who had been mentioned in the king's original list. Mary had been the third and last wife of King Louis XII of France, by whom she had had no children. After the king's death, she had married an Englishman, Charles Brandon, Duke of Suffolk, by whom she had had a son and two daughters. The elder daughter, Frances, had married an Englishman, Henry Grey of Suffolk, by whom she had had one child, a daughter Jane, known to history as Lady Jane Grey. It was she who was listed after King Edward, in place of Princess Mary, on the duke's revised list of successors. In order to bring his own family into the royal succession, the duke managed to arrange a marriage between Lady Jane and his youngest son, Guildford Dudley.

When she learned what had been planned for her, Lady Jane Grey was horrified. She had no desire to be queen and less than no desire to make an enemy of her cousin, Princess Mary. She was, at this time, only sixteen years old; a brilliant student; an expert at languages, including ancient Greek, Latin, and Hebrew; a happy, contented girl without royal ambitions. Tearfully, she begged not to be included in the plan. Northumberland would not listen.

Legally, there was a weakness in the duke's plan. When King Henry VIII had drawn up his original list, he had obtained Parliament's approval before announcing it. It was, therefore, based not only on his authority as king but also on the authority of the lawmaking branch of the government. The duke's list had never had Parliamentary approval. King Edward had intended to call a special meeting for this purpose, but before he could do so his health took a turn for the worse and he died, on July 6, 1553.

Now, King Edward was dead. Like it or not, Lady Jane Grey found herself Queen of England. It is doubtful if, even for a single minute, Lady Jane Grey regarded her elevation to the English throne as lucky. Her abilities and her interests lay in other fields. Once, for example, when her family urged her to join them on a hunt, she gently declined the invitation because she preferred to read one of Plato's works in the original Greek. Said she to a friend: "I fancy all their sport is but a shadow of the pleasure that I find in Plato. Alas, good folks, they never felt what true pleasure means."

Worthy and admirable as she was, Queen Jane never offered a strong appeal to the people of England. A majority of them were Catholics, who had been looking forward to a swing back to their old religion under Catholic Princess Mary. This was one appeal which Queen Jane could not offer to either side in the religious quarrel.

Trouble was in the air, for Princess Mary was most unwilling to give up her right of succession to the throne. Northumberland moved quickly to head it off, but not quite quickly enough. On the morning after King Edward's death, he led a group of troopers out to Hunsdon, where the princess was staying, in order to arrest her and confine her in the Tower. Someone had warned her, and she was gone. Presently, those who favored her began flocking to Suffolk, where she had found refuge in the home of friends. It was not long before she had an army.

In London, troops were gathering to defend Jane's cause, but few of the officers or men felt enthusiasm for this almost-unknown little queen who had suddenly become their Head of State. When it was learned that Princess Mary had established headquarters at a castle on the Suffolk coast, a squadron of warships was sent there to attack. The crews refused to fight against her and joined her cause. Northumberland himself, leading his troops to the attack, confided to Lord Grey, the new queen's father, "The people press to look on us, but no one saith, 'God speed ye!' "

The result could easily have been foretold. Many bodies of Queen's Jane's troops changed sides before a shot had been fired. Northumberland's own men, being led toward battle, halted and refused to advance another step "against our lawful ruler." When it was learned that Princess Mary had declared herself queen and had announced that she would fight for the crown if necessary, almost all of the nobles who had been supporting Queen Jane abandoned her cause. Northumberland himself was one of these, but this traitorous activity availed him nothing, for he and a number of his associates were arrested and thrust into the Tower, to await trial.

One would think that these developments would have filled Queen Jane with despair, but they did not. Never having wanted to be queen, she regarded Princess Mary's advancing forces almost as an army of liberation. When her father—Henry Grey,

Duke of Suffolk—came to her room and informed her that her brief reign was over, she smiled and asked if she might go home now. Alas, it was not that simple. Having been queen, she was regarded as dangerous. She and her husband were arrested and confined in the Tower.

Northumberland, despite his last-minute shift in allegiance, did not escape the axe. When he had been sentenced and had nothing more to lose, he revealed that the Duke of Somerset had been innocent of the charges for which he had been executed the year before. Among Northumberland's associates, also facing death, was Thomas Palmer, the man who had supplied the evidence which had led to Somerset's conviction. Palmer now freely revealed that all of the information about the plots in which the Duke of Somerset was supposed to have taken part had been invented by Northumberland, and that he, Palmer, had memorized it, recited it in court, and sworn to its truth. Even worse, the signature of the dying king on the order for execution had been forged, for the plotters had feared that kind-hearted Edward would refuse to permit the beheading of his former guardian and Lord-Protector.

Princess Mary was crowned Queen of England on September 30, 1553. Like her mother, Catherine of Aragon, she was a profound and very loyal Catholic. One of her first acts, on entering London, had been the release of a large number of Catholic prisoners, including Bishop Gardiner of Winchester, Bishop Bonner of London, and Bishop Tunstall of Durham. It was Bishop Gardiner, newly restored to power, who conducted the religious rites at her coronation.

At first, the new Queen Mary asserted that she would not upset the religious practices of her country. The temptation, though, soon proved too great. In the eyes of the Roman Catholic Church, her father's marriage to her mother was legal, making her legitimate in birth, with a firm claim to the royal succession.

In the eyes of the Church of England, she was the bastard her father had proclaimed her. Presently, she sent quiet word to Pope Julius III that she intended "to restore England to the ancient faith." The Pope was overjoyed. Before long, he felt the time was ripe to send the exiled Cardinal Pole back to England.

At the time of her coronation, Queen Mary was thirty-seven years old but looked a great deal older. Her reddish hair was stringy and streaked with gray. A variety of illnesses and injustices had not been good to her. Her face was a network of wrinkles, her eyes were weak, and her voice was husky. In most respects she was a reasonable person, but absolute certainty that her religion was right made her intolerant of anyone whose beliefs differed from hers. In this, she was urged on by her kinsman, Emperor Charles V, who was as fanatical a Catholic as she.

From the emperor, she received a list of names of people to be put to death, for religious and other reasons. It was not a long list, and many of the names on it seemed reasonable enough for execution—such leaders and misleaders as Northumberland, Palmer, and others of the sort. One name, though, was startling —that of her half sister Elizabeth! Elizabeth was as strong a Protestant as Mary was Catholic. Not to be would be to deny the rightness of King Henry's divorce from Catherine of Aragon, which would automatically rule out the lawfulness of her mother's marriage to the king and make her illegitimate. Nevertheless, Princess Elizabeth suddenly declared herself a Catholic, attending Mass regularly and even sending for a cross, a chalice, and other items connected with the Catholic ceremony. This may not have deceived Queen Mary, but at least it gave the queen an excuse to preserve her half sister's life.

The emperor also sent Queen Mary a letter urging her immediate marriage to a Catholic prince. Children would be necessary to establish a new, strong, Catholic line on the English throne.

Regretting that his age and the state of his health ruled him out as a candidate, he nominated his son, King Philip II of Spain. Philip was a young and handsome man, a full ten years younger than Mary, but he was willing to obey his father and marry the Queen of England. Such a match might leave much to be desired romantically, but it held great possible gains for the Holy Roman Empire, for Spain, and for the ruling House of Hapsburg, to which both Emperor Charles and King Philip belonged.

Announcement of Queen Mary's engagement to King Philip II of Spain caused great excitement throughout England. Protestants were especially upset, for the marriage of these two strongly Catholic rulers seemed more than likely to bring the end of any Protestant worship in the country. Many Catholics were also distressed, for the danger seemed great that England and her people would come under the control of the Spanish royal family, thus bringing an end to English independence.

The immediate result was violence. In four different parts of the country, groups of plotters had been quietly at work, organizing forces to be used when and if a cause would be right and conditions favorable for an armed overthrow of Queen Mary's government. The exciting news triggered the revolts too early. Fighting broke out in Wales, where Sir James Croft led forth his armed peasant tenants; in Devonshire, under Sir Peter Carew; in Kent, under Sir Thomas Wyatt the Younger, son of the famous poet; and in Warwickshire, under Lady Jane Grey's father, the Duke of Suffolk.

Members of the Queen's Council panicked, fearing to oppose the rebels, but the queen herself showed that she was made of stronger stuff. Learning that the London Assembly was holding a meeting at the Guildhall to determine which side to favor, she went there in person and addressed the members. Knowing that it was her plan to marry King Philip that had brought on the revolts, she promised that if the members of the House of

Commons should vote against the Spanish marriage she would obey their wishes and, indeed, would live the rest of her life alone, without a husband, if they wanted that. She added, though, that she would not let objection to her marriage serve as "a Spanish cloak" for a revolt of discontented people against her rule, and she promised to love and to favor her people.

The queen's words encouraged the Assembly and the members of Parliament to support her cause. Strong bands of troops were quickly gathered and sent out against the rebels. Faced with such strong opposition, three of the four revolts collapsed. Sir Peter Carew and Sir James Croft abandoned their troops and fled. The Duke of Suffolk was arrested and confined to the Tower, where his daughter and his son-in-law had been for many months. Only Sir Thomas Wyatt continued on.

Wyatt and his fifteen thousand followers made a tough fight of it. Against odds of nearly two to one, they entered London and fought their way almost to the palace at Whitehall. A reward of a thousand pounds was offered to any man who should take the young leader prisoner. Hearing of this, Wyatt wore his name in large letters, "fair written, on his cap," to guide anyone who dared try to take him. There was fear that he and his men might capture the queen, but they failed by a narrow margin. Wyatt himself was taken, and the Tower received another "guest." A knight, Sir Maurice Berkeley, received the thousand pounds.

The rebellions were followed by tragedy and near-tragedy. The fact that the Duke of Suffolk was one of the leaders cast added suspicion on his daughter, Queen Jane, and her husband. Two orders of execution were written out, one for Henry Grey, Duke of Suffolk, the other for "Guildford Dudley and his wife." Knowing that she and her husband were to die, Jane Grey nevertheless refused to see him, for fear that one or both would break down in the presence of their enemies. "We shall meet soon enough in the other world," she said with determination.

On the morning of February 12, 1554, Guildford Dudley was taken out and publicly beheaded on Tower Hill. From her window, Jane watched him go and watched his body brought back. Then the little seventeen-year-old "nine-days Queen" was taken down to an execution dungeon in the Tower, so that people would not see how young and innocent she looked. After a few short prayers, she turned to the headsman and said, "I pray you dispatch me quickly." She was then blindfolded, and with some help and guidance she placed her head on the block. "Lord! Into thy hands I commend my spirit." A single, quick blow severed her neck and ended her life.

On that same day, forty-eight captured rebels were publicly hanged from gibbets erected about the city of London. Five days later, some twenty or thirty suffered a similar fate in Kent. On the twenty-third, Queen Jane's father, the Duke of Suffolk, was beheaded. The next day, the ambassador from the Holy Roman Empire wrote to Charles V: "The Queen has granted a general pardon to a multitude of people, after having caused about five score of the most guilty to be executed."

One who had not yet been either executed or pardoned was young Thomas Wyatt. Queen Mary could not avoid the suspicion that Princess Elizabeth and Sir Edward Courtenay were involved in Wyatt's bold attempt against her life, a feeling which was kept very much alive by repeated messages from Emperor Charles V, urging their execution. Wyatt was secretly offered his own life in return for evidence of the guilt of the princess and her friend. Wyatt was tempted and made a few vague statements that seemed to indicate their guilt, but in the end he could not bring himself to implicate innocent people. In his final testimony, he declared that neither of them knew anything of the plot. He was hanged. Their lives were spared, but they remained prisoners in the Tower.

It has been said that the revolts of 1553/1554 mark the dividing line between the reigns of "Gentle Queen Mary" and "Bloody Mary." While it is true that the revolts did convince her that she had been too gentle with those who wished her ill, neither her activities before nor those after the revolts seem to justify the adjective "bloody" for her, as compared to other monarchs of her time. The mid-sixteenth century was not a gentle period.

As the time for her marriage approached, Queen Mary became increasingly worried lest her careworn appearance should repel her prospective husband, who had not yet come from Spain and had never seen her. She was beginning to think that he had no intention of coming when, on July 19, 1554, he landed at Southampton. At once, the anxious queen started south to meet him. They met at Winchester, where they were married on July 25 by Bishop Gardiner. After a few days there, they proceeded on to Windsor Palace. The people saw very little of them.

It was Queen Mary's belief that the most important single thing she could do for her country, her people, and her own immortal soul would be to return England to the Roman Catholic Church, with all religious matters completely under the control of the Pope. This would take a good deal of doing. Throughout England were many great lords and other landowners who had gained valuable parts of their property through the seizing or purchase of Church lands. Since the return of the Catholic Church to power in England might well result in the loss of these lands, these men would not be likely to support such a change. There was also the question of Parliament, without whose cooperation such a change would have no legal standing. How could the support of Parliament be guaranteed?

The landowners were won over through a strong appeal by Bishop Gardiner to Pope Julius III. Convinced after some hesitation, the Pope issued a papal bull, or pronouncement, officially "giving, alienating, and transferring" to those presently holding

them all lands which had been taken from the Roman Catholic
Church during the reigns of King Henry VIII and King Edward
VI. The landowners were delighted. No longer would they have
to worry that the Church would some day take back the lands.
They now had an ironclad title to their property, given them by
the Pope himself, and they were anxious to show their gratitude.

Parliament was a different matter. Many members of the
House of Lords had been won over by the Pope's proclamation
so there was nothing to fear from that body. Few members of
the House of Commons, though, were landowners, and a good
percentage were Protestants. There was no assurance that a bill
to return to the Church of Rome would pass in that body. Consequently, the queen ordered a new election and sent word to the
county sheriffs, who supervised the voting, that no one who
was not a Roman Catholic was to be elected. In one way or
another, the sheriffs accomplished what they had been told to
do, with the result that a solidly Catholic House of Commons
was elected.

So the English Church returned to the arms of Rome. In the
House of Lords, the return to Catholicism was carried by acclaim,
without a single dissenting voice. There was some slight opposition in the House of Commons. Of the 300 members, 298 either
spoke in favor of the return to Rome or remained silent. Two did
raise their voices in opposition, but when the time to vote arrived, the next day, all 300 voted in favor of reuniting. By that
time, the daring two had come to realize what would doubtless
happen to them if they persisted in saying what they thought.

The official ceremony of return took place on November 30,
1554. Queen Mary sat on her throne, with King Philip on her
left hand and Cardinal Pole on her right. Before her were the
members of Parliament and some few important guests. The
official petition for return to Rome was read aloud, after which
the cardinal officially absolved "all those present, and the whole

nation, and the dominions thereof from all heresy and schism [division] and all judgments, censures, and penalties for that cause incurred." He then restored them "to the communion of Holy Church in the name of the Father, Son, and Holy Ghost." A bill was then passed granting to the Pope all of the powers that he had had in England before King Henry VIII had removed the Church in England from the authority of Rome.

It should be noted that Cardinal Pole's absolving of the people from heresy and schism and the penalties for these applied only to past offenses. It was clear that those who had been so absolved had better not do it again. To make this doubly clear, Parliament presently passed a very strict law against heresy.

There followed a three-year period of religious persecution. Cardinal Pole did his best to make it a period of gentle persuasion, but Queen Mary and such fanatics as Bishops Gardiner, Bonner, and Thirlby—who had been made to suffer imprisonment while the Protestants were in power—were strongly in favor of the immediate stamping out of heresy. Approximately three hundred people were burned at the stake, four being leading Protestant churchmen: Bishops Hooper, Ridley, and Latimer, and Archbishop Cranmer.

The case of Archbishop Cranmer was an especially unhappy occasion. He had been told repeatedly that if he would renounce his heresies and return to the Church, he would be forgiven. The thought of the flames terrified him, and at last he agreed to recant, writing out a long and involved series of statements favoring the Catholic forms of worship over those he had helped introduce in the Church of England. Queen Mary received his recantations but chose not to believe them and sent to Rome for permission to burn him. This was necessary because he held such high Church office. Two popes—Julius III and Marcellus II—died in 1555 while the matter was under consideration, but this did Archbishop Cranmer no good. The next pope, Paul IV, was the least tolerant of the three and sent the permission through on December 4, soon after taking office.

Archbishop Cranmer was led out to execution on March 21, 1556. He was fastened to the stake, and the fire was lighted. Before he died, he made sure that all present knew that he was ashamed of having recanted his beliefs in a vain effort to save his life. As the flames mounted, he held his right hand in the midst of the fire, crying out, "Forasmuch as my hand offended, writing contrary to my heart, my hand shall first be punished. It shall be first burned." Steadfastly and without flinching, he held his hand in the midst of the fire until it was consumed. Soon thereafter, he was dead. John Foxe, in his *Book of Martyrs*, states that when the fire had died down, Cranmer's heart was found, whole and undamaged, among the ashes.

King Philip has an unpleasant reputation among Protestants for his intolerance toward heretics, but during the persecutions in Queen Mary's reign he did some things, at least, to establish a kinder verdict. It was through his influence that Princess Elizabeth and Sir Edward Courtenay were freed from their imprisonment. On another occasion, he overruled one of the bishops who had recommended a large group of Protestants for destruction and, instead, set them free.

King Philip's stay in England could hardly have been very enjoyable for him. He was married to an unattractive, unwell, and intolerant wife who was ten years older than he. He stayed with her, though, for thirteen months, hoping, as she did, that she would conceive a boy baby who could be brought up as a Catholic and would follow her on the throne. Twice, it was thought that the queen was pregnant, but each time it proved to be a false hope, brought on by her bad health. She herself laid her failure to her lack of zeal in punishing the Protestants, but there were not many people at home or abroad who would have agreed that she had sinned in that particular way.

King Philip made one more visit to England, though it was hardly a heart-directed call upon the woman he loved. In 1557, his country of Spain was at war with France, and he came over in March of that year to try to convince Queen Mary to join him in a war against the common enemy. He was successful. Anxious to please her husband, Queen Mary used her influence to get Parliament to declare war on the French. An army of ten thousand English soldiers went to the Netherlands, under the Earl of Pembroke, and the English fleet made a series of attacks on French seaports. It was all in vain, doubly so! Queen Mary was not able to tempt King Philip to come back to her, nor were the two of them able to win the war. While the English troops were helping the Spaniards on the mainland and the English navy was raiding, the Duke of Guise led a French army in a surprise attack on Calais and the neighboring English-held towns and captured them in January 1558. Soon thereafter, King Philip made a separate peace with the French, gaining for himself the best terms he could but not even discussing the return of Calais to the English, who had held it for 211 years. This was a sad blow to English prestige and to Queen Mary herself. Said she: "When I am dead and opened, ye shall find Calais lying in my heart."

Queen Mary did not live out the year of 1558. During the late summer, she became ill with "an ague fever," and on November 17 she died. On the very next day, Cardinal Pole died of the very same type of fever, which had been raging as an epidemic throughout England. Sick as he was, he had continued to persecute and condemn heretics. Five of them, three men and two women, had been burned at the stake within the few days preceding the cardinal's death.

With the deaths of the queen and the cardinal, their policy of persecuting people for their religion was proved to have been a terrible mistake. Not only the Protestants but also most of the

Catholics had been experiencing a growing horror at the steady parade of victims to the flames. Never after that time were the English people willing to renew the control of the Papacy over their land. The Catholic churchmen and their queen had defeated their own cause.

On the original list of succession drawn up by King Henry VIII, his daughter Elizabeth was to follow her half sister Mary on the English throne. There had been periods during Queen Mary's rule when it had seemed most unlikely that such a thing would ever occur. Mary was an ardent Catholic, Elizabeth a Protestant. Mary was a champion of religious learning and teaching, Elizabeth of secular knowledge. Mary was fanatical, Elizabeth tolerant. Though Elizabeth had sided with Mary during the nine days' reign of Queen Jane Grey in 1553 and had refused to lend any support to Wyatt's rebellion the following year, she had been confined at Hatfield under the guardianship of Sir Thomas Pope because Queen Mary regarded her as dangerous.

Not until Queen Mary's death late in 1558 was the true nature of Elizabeth's "danger" fully revealed. It was popularity. An English public, weary of religious persecution under Queen Mary and her heretic-hunting clergymen, longed for a more tolerant ruler of Princess Elizabeth's mold. No sooner had Queen Mary died than both houses of Parliament—Catholics and Protestants alike—proclaimed Elizabeth Queen. For a while, it was hard to find a bishop to crown her, for most churchmen felt that crowning a Protestant Queen of England might lead to religious uprisings, but on January 15, 1559, the Bishop of Carlisle reluctantly consented to do so, and did. There were no uprisings.

Parliament went into session ten days after the coronation. The members of both houses showed their trust in their queen by unanimously declaring her "the lawful, undoubted, and true heir to the Crown, lawfully descended from the blood-royal," thus establishing beyond any question her right to be queen and her prized legitimacy. She was also given the title of Supreme Governess of the Church of England, with the same religious powers that her father and her brother had exercised.

Early in her reign, Queen Elizabeth was faced with a variety of foreign problems which presented threats to her country. The first was the war with France, which had begun during Queen Mary's reign and had gone badly for England when the Duke of Guise took Calais. King Philip II of Spain, who had reached satisfactory terms of peace between his own country and France, offered to continue to fight against the French with the thought of helping recover Calais provided Elizabeth would guarantee to keep England in the war for another six years. Wisely, Elizabeth refused this great drain and strain upon her country, even though the best separate treaty she could make with King Henry II of France would mean the permanent loss of Calais and all of the English area lying about it on the French coast.

Elizabeth's next international problem was a personal one involving King Philip II of Spain. He had been the husband of her half sister Mary; now he wanted to marry her. After carefully considering the hold on her country which such a union would give to Spain, she declined the king's offer and elected to remain an unmarried woman, though she was still only twenty-five years old.

One of the most heartrending and potentially dangerous situations which Queen Elizabeth had to face concerned a cousin, Queen Mary of Scotland—the famous Mary, Queen of Scots. Mary was the granddaughter of King Henry VIII's older sister, Margaret, who had become Queen of Scotland when she had married King James IV of that country. Mary had become queen at the age of six days, when her father, King James V, died in 1542. A revolt in 1568 forced her to flee across the English

Elizabeth I, Queen of England and Ireland from 1558 to 1603. (The "Armada" portrait by Marcus Gheeraerts II)

border and to appeal to Queen Elizabeth for protection, and thus her little boy became King James VI of Scotland at the age of two.

Mary, Queen of Scots, was not a comfortable sort of guest to have. Being a member of the English royal family of Tudor—a direct descendant of King Henry VII—she had a claim of her own to the crown of England and might, at any time, prove to be a dangerous rival to Queen Elizabeth. The fact that Mary was a Catholic while Elizabeth was a Protestant added peril to the situation, making them natural opponents in any religious strife that might arise. At the insistence of her Council members, Queen Elizabeth had her guest imprisoned in Carlisle Castle, where, it was felt, she could do little harm.

There was no shortage of damaging stories told about Queen Mary of Scotland. Most of them have never definitely been proved or disproved. For example, it was said that she had guilty knowledge of the plan to murder her unpopular second husband, Lord Darnley, and perhaps had even helped work out the details. She was also thought to be connected with the infamous Babington plot, a conspiracy by a group of Catholic nobles who were said to be planning to assassinate Queen Elizabeth, overthrow her Protestant regime, and give England a Catholic government with Mary as Queen. Rumors such as these were made all the more terrifying by letters such as the one written from Paris by Sir Henry Norris to Elizabeth's chief minister William Cecil, warning that "the Queen's Majesty doth now hold the wolf that would devour her. . . . It is conspired betwixt the King of Spain, the Pope, and the French King that the Queen's Majesty shall be destroyed, whereby the Queen of Scots may succeed Her Majesty."

One result of the series of disquieting accusations was a change of prisons for the Scottish Queen, from reasonably comfortable and accessible Carlisle Castle to remote Bolton Castle, in northern Yorkshire, where it would be much more difficult for any unauthorized person to visit her. Another result was that a trial was held to sift the evidence and determine her actual guilt. In September, 1586—after eighteen years of imprisonment as Queen Elizabeth's "guest"—Mary was declared guilty. A month later, she was condemned to death. Queen Elizabeth, reluctant to execute her unhappy kinswoman, delayed the signing of the execution order as long as she could, but at last, on February 1, 1587, after repeated insistence by Lord Cecil, she signed it. A week later, the headsman earned his fee.

Queen Elizabeth was one of England's greatest rulers. Though the birth of a girl child to Queen Anne Boleyn had discouraged King Henry VIII, he need not really have worried at all. In mind and in character, she was far more like a man than a woman, and what little she may have lacked in kingly attributes she more than made up by the highly qualified men with whom she surrounded herself. We have already met her chief minister, William Cecil, Lord Burghley. Outstanding among the many others always at her beck and call were Sir Francis Walsingham, the architect of the very efficient English spy system that kept the queen informed in advance of every foregin danger, and Sir Walter Raleigh, famous in legend for having spread his cloak in the mud for his queen to walk upon but far more deserving of fame for his explorations and colonization in the New World of the Americas.

Dashing and spectacular as was King Henry VIII in tournament and on battlefield, and impressive as were such of his experimental warships as the *"Great Harry,"* it was his daughter Elizabeth—the despised, the "illegitimate"—who molded England into a single nation and raised it to the status of a world power. Instead of switching irresponsibly back and forth between Catholicism and Protestantism, first persecuting one group and then the other in an attempt to strike a balance, she let her people set their own pattern through the actions of their Parliament, resulting in a tolerant government that permitted both forms of worship, within a Protestant framework, without persecuting either. A most desirable by-product of this was the development of a strong national spirit. The English people became unified, ready to act together in behalf of their island country.

With the possible exception of the new national spirit, without which nothing could have been done to develop England into a world power, the most important single factor was the development of the English navy. Though not herself a sailor, Queen Elizabeth saw to it that her nation's sea power was in the competent hands of those who knew all that was to be known of warships and their uses. It is doubtful if any nation at any time has had more competent naval leadership than did Queen Elizabeth's England. It was well that this was so, for the ships and men were to be needed and needed desperately.

King Philip II of Spain was the principal source of danger. Distressed by his loss of a claim to the English throne through the death of his wife; angered by Queen Elizabeth's refusal of his offer to marry her; and horrified by the execution of the Catholic Mary, Queen of Scots, he was laying careful plans for the conquest of England and the dethroning of the island country's Protestant queen. Work was started on the collecting and constructing of a vast fleet to sweep the English navy from the seas and land a Spanish army on the English shore. The projected time of attack was the fall of 1587.

As soon as the menace was known, Elizabeth's English seamen moved to counter it. Cadiz harbor was crowded with Spanish vessels, preparing for the invasion. Though Spain and England were still technically at peace, Sir Francis Drake boldly led a fleet of twenty-three English warships into Cadiz harbor, capturing or destroying everything he could. For thirty-four hours, he rampaged around one of the most strongly fortified harbors on the Spanish coast, sinking thirty-one major Spanish warships and numerous smaller ones without the loss of a single English ship. When at last he departed, he had with him six captured vessels, heavily laden with supplies and treasure. Said Drake, "I have singed the beard of the King of Spain." He had, indeed! As a result of his raid, the invasion had to be postponed almost a year.

The Invincible Spanish Armada, as King Philip's mighty fleet was called, at last put to sea on May 30, 1588, under the command of the young Duke of Medina-Sidonia. At Calais, it was to pick up the Duke of Parma and his Spanish army of seventeen thousand veteran troops and ferry them to the English coast, where they were to land and begin conquering. It was hard to see what England could do to stave off this mighty force of 137 armed vessels, including some of the greatest warships in the world.

The English had only about half as many ships of war, and these averaged considerably smaller than their Spanish opponents. They had, however, four of the most experienced and daring seamen of the age: Lord High Admiral Charles Howard, Vice Admiral Sir Francis Drake, Sir John Hawkins, and Sir Martin Frobisher. On July 29, 1588, as the Spanish Armada approached their shores, these four men took their modest navy out and began nibbling at the fringes of the crescent formation, in which the Spaniards were sailing. Long-range bombardment from upwind and sudden, concentrated attacks on separated Spanish units were their two most useful and most used maneuvers. After a week of such intermittent small-scale fighting, Lord High Admiral Howard was able to write to Queen Elizabeth: "Their force is wonderful, great and strong; and yet we pluck their feathers, by little and little."

At last, the unhappy Duke of Medina-Sidonia managed to bring his Armada into the harbor of Calais and anchor there.

Parma and his army had not yet arrived. There was nothing to do but wait, but the Spaniards were not allowed to wait. That night, eight old English vessels sailed into the harbor, each one furiously ablaze. At Antwerp, three years before, the Spaniards had met fireships whose holds were packed with high explosives, able to spread destruction over wide areas when they exploded. Here, it seemed, were more "Antwerp hell-burners." There was no time to haul up anchors. The cables were hastily cut, sails were raised, and each ship of the Armada did its best to avoid the dreaded fireships and reach the safety of the open sea. One galleon ran aground, but the others all got safely away, while the fireships sailed to the shore, and burned. There had been no explosives after all!

Out into the North Sea went the Armada, still chivied along by its persistent English enemies. Being without their anchors, the ships were now in great danger from storms, for they could not anchor and ride them out. There was no longer a thought of invading England. Escape was now the important project. Past the northern coast of Scotland went the Armada, out into the Atlantic, then south toward Spain. Fifty of the Spanish ships managed to reach home; eighty-seven did not. It was one of the greatest of naval disasters.

Wrote Sir Francis Drake, in his report of the affair: "With all their great and terrible ostentation, they did not, in all their sailing round about England, so much as sink or take one ship, barque, pinnace, or cock-boat of ours, or even burn so much as one sheep-cote on this land."

Even when they won a naval battle, the Spaniards seemed to lose more than they gained. In 1591, the English warship *Revenge* was cornered in the Azores Islands by a Spanish squadron of fifty-three vessels, of which fifteen were larger warships than she was. In spite of the odds, Sir Richard Grenville elected to fight to the death. Fifteen hours later, the *Revenge* was still fighting, though Grenville and most of his men were dead. Three of the enemy ships had gone down, and the rest had been badly battered. Boarders took the *Revenge*, but it did them little good. When the Spanish squadron was overtaken by a hurricane, some days later, the little English ship went down, as did all of the battered Spanish ships against which she had been fighting.

The war against Spain went on until Philip II died in 1598. By that time, once-mighty Spain was through as a sea power, and England had become the Number One naval nation of the world. While it may be accurate to speak of King Henry VIII as the Father of the English Navy, we must recognize that it was his unwanted daughter Elizabeth who used her country's naval strength to raise England to the status of a world power.

It was not only in war and in naval affairs that Queen Elizabeth helped guide England toward greatness. Hers was a period of colonization and colonial expansion, under the leadership of such able men as Sir Walter Raleigh. Industry flourished. So did literature, with such poets as Christopher Marlowe, Edmund Spenser, Francis Beaumont, and John Fletcher, some of whom also wrote plays; such dramatists as Ben Jonson and William Shakespeare, who also wrote poems; and such a philosopher as Francis Bacon. It was an age of awakening, of thought, and of creativity. Under Elizabeth, England rose to the top level of nations.

As it must to all people, death came to Queen Elizabeth in 1603. She had never married and had no descendants to follow her on the throne. Her sister Mary had left no descendants, either, nor had her brother Edward. Who, then, should follow her as ruler of England?

There was only one possible answer. James Stuart—King James VI of Scotland—was the only relative near enough for serious consideration. So the son of Mary, Queen of Scots, was freely granted the throne over which his mother had been executed. James VI of Scotland became also James I of England, thus uniting the two kingdoms. He was followed by his son Charles I in 1625, then (after an eleven-year "protectorate" under Oliver and Richard Cromwell, 1649–1660) by his two grandsons, Charles II, in 1660, and James II, in 1685.

James II, a devout Catholic, made the mistake of trying to enforce his religion on his English subjects. He was forced out in in a bloodless revolt, the Glorious Revolution of 1688. To replace him, Parliament selected two-rulers, James's Protestant daughter Mary and her husand, William, ruler of the Netherlands. Queen Mary died in 1701 and King William in 1702. They were followed on the throne by Mary's sister Anne. During her reign, in 1707, England and Scotland were united into a single nation, known as Great Britain. When Queen Anne died in 1714, the crown went to George, the son of her German cousin Sophia. Ever since that time, the direct descendants of King George I have occupied the British throne.

# BIBLIOGRAPHY

Bragdon, Henry W. "Thomas Cranmer, Doctor of Divinity: A Study in Misunderstanding." Thesis for Distinction in the Field of English History and Literature, Harvard University, 1928.

Burnet, Gilbert. *History of the Reformation of the Church of England*. Oxford: Clarendon Press, 1875.

Creighton, Mandell. *Cardinal Wolsey*. London: Macmillan, 1888.

Dixon, R. W. *The History of the Church of England from the Abolition of the Roman Jurisdiction*. London: Smith, Elder & Co., 1878.

Durant, Will. *The Reformation*. The Story of Civilization, vol. 6. New York: Simon and Schuster, 1957.

Fattorusso, Joseph and Rita. *A Genealogical Chronological History of the Kings and Queens of England and France*. Medici Historical Atlases, vols. 1 and 2. Florence: 1953.

Fisher, M. A. L. *The Political History of England*. Vol. 5. London: Longmans Green, 1919.

Froude, J. A. *History of England from the Fall of Wolsey to the Death of Elizabeth*. London: Parker, 1856.

Green, John Richard. *A Short History of the English People*. Vol. 2. New York: Harper and Brothers, 1893.

Hackett, Francis. *Henry the Eighth*. New York: Liveright Publishing Corp., 1929, 1945.

Hamilton, Julia. *Anne of Cleves.* New York: Beagle Books, Inc., 1972.

Lingard, John. *The History of England.* London: Dolman, 1849.

Luke, Mary M. *Catherine the Queen.* New York: Coward, McCann, Inc., 1967.

Morrison, N. Brysson. *The Private Life of Henry VIII.* New York: Vanguard Press, 1964.

Pollard, A. F. *Henry VIII.* London: Goupil & Co., 1902.

Rival, Paul. *The Six Wives of Henry VIII.* New York: G. P. Putnam's Sons, 1936.

Scarisbrick, J. J. *Henry VIII.* Berkeley and Los Angeles: University of California Press, 1968.

Smyth, C. M. *Cranmer and the Reformation under Edward VI.* Cambridge: Cambridge University Press, 1926.

Southworth, John V. D. *The Age of Sails.* War at Sea, vol. 2. New York: Twayne Publishers, 1968.

————. *The Story of the World.* New York: Pocket Books, Inc., 1954.

Time–Life Books. *The Age of Faith, The Age of Enlightenment, The Reformation.* New York: Time-Life Books, 1968–1971.

Williams, Henry Smith. *The Historians' History of the World.* Vol. 19. London and New York: Encyclopaedia Britannica, Inc., 1926.

Williams, Neville. *Henry VIII and His Court.* New York: Macmillan, 1971.

# INDEX

*Italic figures denote illustrations*